ROS2 and Python in Action

Building Intelligent Robots for Navigation, Sensing, and Real-World Problem Solving

Thompson Carter

Rafael Sanders

Miguel Farmer

Contents

How to Scan a Barcode to Get a Repository

1. **Install a QR/Barcode Scanner** - Ensure you have a barcode or QR code scanner app installed on your smartphone or use a built-in scanner in **GitHub, GitLab, or Bitbucket.**

2. **Open the Scanner** - Launch the scanner app and grant necessary camera permissions.

3. **Scan the Barcode** - Align the barcode within the scanning frame. The scanner will automatically detect and process it.

4. **Follow the Link** - The scanned result will display a **URL to the repository.** Tap the link to open it in your web browser or Git client.

5. **Clone the Repository** - Use **Git clone** with the provided URL to download the repository to your local machine.

Chapter 1: Introduction to ROS2 and Python

Welcome to the first chapter of this comprehensive guide on ROS2 (Robot Operating System 2) and Python. As you embark on your journey into modern robotics, you'll discover how these two powerful tools combine to create intelligent, autonomous systems capable of navigating complex environments and performing tasks that push the boundaries of innovation. In this chapter, we will lay the foundation for everything you need to know before diving deeper into the subsequent chapters. We'll begin by exploring why robotics is such a hot topic today, then give you a concise overview of ROS2, highlight Python's importance in this field, survey some exciting real-world applications, and finally discuss the structure of this book so you can get the most out of every section.

By the end of this chapter, you'll understand the "why" behind robotics, have a grasp of what ROS2 is all about, see why Python is a go-to language for robotics, explore the most interesting real-world use cases, and know precisely how to navigate this book. Let's get started.

1.1. Why Robotics? Why Now?

Robotics has transitioned from the realm of science fiction into an integral part of daily life and industrial processes. Whether it's self-driving cars, robotic arms in factories, or drones delivering packages, robots are becoming more prevalent and accessible. But **why is robotics experiencing such rapid growth today**? And **why should you, as a learner or professional, care about it now** more than ever?

Below are some key factors driving the rise of robotics:

1. **Advancements in Computing**
    - **Affordable Hardware**: Over the past decade, the cost of powerful single-board computers (like the Raspberry Pi) and microcontrollers (like the Arduino) has plummeted. This means you can get started with robotics without a massive budget.
    - **Graphical Processing Units (GPUs)**: The increased use of GPUs for parallel processing has accelerated machine learning and computer vision, allowing robots to "see" and "think" more effectively.
    - **Edge Computing**: Instead of offloading all computations to a remote data center, devices can now process data on-site, reducing latency and improving real-time decision-making.
2. **Ease of Development**

- **Open-Source Ecosystems**: From Linux to ROS (Robot Operating System) and Python libraries, open-source software has made it simpler for developers and enthusiasts to build on existing tools without reinventing the wheel.
- **Community Support**: Large online communities provide tutorials, forums, troubleshooting guides, and collaborative projects that speed up the learning curve.

3. **Industry Demands**
   - **Automation for Efficiency**: Many industries—such as manufacturing, logistics, and healthcare—seek to automate repetitive tasks, reduce human error, and handle labor-intensive work more safely.
   - **New Frontiers**: Space exploration agencies are developing advanced rovers and robotic arms to operate in the harsh environment of other planets or asteroids, driving innovation and capturing the public imagination.
4. **Multidisciplinary Collaboration**
   - **Convergence of Fields**: Robotics intersects mechanical engineering, electrical engineering, computer science, and artificial intelligence. This intersection fosters fresh ideas and solutions for complex challenges.

- **Educational Focus:** Schools and universities now offer specialized programs and courses in robotics, expanding the talent pool.

5. **COVID-19 Aftermath**
    - **Contactless Operations:** The global pandemic amplified the need for minimal human contact in certain tasks (delivering groceries, medical supplies, etc.). Robots can reduce the risk of infection and operate around the clock.

Consider this: ***What was once expensive and cutting-edge is now affordable, well-documented, and supported by a thriving community.*** *If you've ever toyed with the idea of building or programming a robot, there has never been a better time to dive in.*

Diagram 1.1: Robotics Timeline

To illustrate the evolution of robotics, imagine a simple timeline:

```
1950s    1960s    1970s    1980s    1990s    2000s    2010s    2020s
  |        |        |        |        |        |        |        |
Birth    Early    Industrial  Rise of  Growth  Advent   AI &    Explosion
of         space    robotics     personal  of        of        ML        of
modern     race      in factories computing internet  advanced      robotics
computing                                              robotics
```

This simplified timeline underscores that robotics, once a niche domain of large corporations and government labs, has become democratized. You're tapping into a rich heritage that started with basic mechanical automation and has flourished into advanced, networked, and AI-driven machines.

Key Takeaway: *Robotics is not just a futuristic fantasy—it's a rapidly expanding field where your contributions can have a tangible, immediate impact. Whether you're a hobbyist or a professional, mastering ROS2 and Python grants you the power to build or refine robots with real-world applications.*

1.2. Introducing ROS2: A Quick Overview

The **Robot Operating System (ROS)** has been one of the most groundbreaking developments in robotics for over a decade. Now in its second major iteration—aptly named **ROS2**—this set of software libraries and tools has been redesigned to meet the demands of the next generation of robotics. But what exactly is ROS2, and **why should you care**?

1.2.1 The Essence of ROS2

In the simplest terms, ROS2 is a **middleware**: It's the glue that holds together different components of a robot's software, such as drivers, algorithms, and user interfaces.

While it's often called an operating system, it doesn't replace your primary OS (Ubuntu, Windows, or macOS). Instead, it provides a robust framework for organizing and orchestrating robotic components.

At a high level, ROS2 includes:

- **Communication Tools**: Publishers, subscribers, services, actions, and more to facilitate data exchange among various parts of a robot.
- **Packages and Libraries**: Ready-made modules for navigation, perception, manipulation, and other common robotic tasks.
- **Build and Launch System**: Tools for compiling ROS2 packages and easily starting multiple nodes (programs) in a single command.
- **Community**: A vast ecosystem of contributors who create and maintain packages, documentation, and tutorials.

1.2.2 Why ROS2 Instead of ROS1?

ROS1 was and still is highly popular, but it had limitations:

1. **Single-Threaded**: Many of its core systems were not designed for multi-threading, hindering real-time performance.
2. **Platform Constraints**: ROS1 was primarily geared towards Ubuntu Linux.

3. **Real-Time Support:** Industrial and safety-critical applications needed better real-time capabilities.
4. **Reliability and Security:** As robots move into production environments—like factories or healthcare facilities—robust security and fault tolerance became critical.

ROS2 addresses these challenges by leveraging **DDS (Data Distribution Service)**, which supports reliable, multi-platform communication, real-time capabilities, and more advanced security features. This means that if you want to build a robot capable of working in a high-stakes environment—or you simply want a more future-proof platform—ROS2 is the clear choice.

1.2.3 Key Concepts in ROS2

To understand how ROS2 actually works, let's break down some core concepts:

1. **Nodes**
    - A **node** is a single executable that performs a specific task. For example, one node might handle camera input, while another node might process sensor data for navigation.
    - Nodes promote modularity and allow you to distribute tasks across multiple machines or processors.
2. **Topics**

- **Topics** are named communication channels through which nodes exchange messages.
- A node that sends out data (like sensor readings) is a **publisher**, while a node that receives data (like an algorithm that processes those readings) is a **subscriber**.

3. **Services**

   - While topics handle continuous streams of data, **services** are used for request/response interactions. For instance, you might call a service to move a robotic arm to a specific position.

4. **Actions**

   - **Actions** allow for preemptable, long-running tasks. If you need your robot to perform a complex maneuver that takes several seconds or minutes, an action can provide feedback and allow cancellation mid-operation.

5. **Parameters**

   - **Parameters** let you configure nodes at runtime. This is handy for tasks like adjusting camera exposure or changing a robot's speed without recompiling your code.

1.2.4 Getting Started with ROS2

If you're new to ROS2, here's a quick **step-by-step** overview of how you might get started:

1. **Choose an OS**: While ROS2 supports multiple platforms, Ubuntu (often the Long-Term Support version) is commonly recommended for beginners.
2. **Install Dependencies:** This includes Python, development tools like CMake, and any hardware drivers you need.
3. **Install ROS2**: Follow the official ROS2 installation steps for your specific distribution (e.g., ROS2 Humble, Iron, etc.).
4. **Create a Workspace**: Typically a directory where all your ROS2 packages and source code will live.
5. **Use the CLI Tools**: Familiarize yourself with commands like ros2 node list, ros2 topic echo, or ros2 launch to manage nodes and topics.
6. **Experiment with Tutorials**: Official ROS2 tutorials demonstrate how to write and run your own publisher-subscriber nodes.

Each of these steps will be covered in detail in later chapters, but for now, keep in mind that **ROS2 is your toolbox** for managing all the moving parts of your robot's software architecture.

1.3. The Power of Python in Robotics

With a vast array of programming languages available–C++, Java, MATLAB, and more–**why does Python reign supreme** in the field of robotics, especially when paired with ROS2?

1.3.1 Python's Core Strengths

1. **Simplicity and Readability**
    - Python's clean and intuitive syntax makes it easy for beginners to read and write code. This reduces the learning curve and allows you to focus on robotic logic rather than language intricacies.
2. **Rich Ecosystem of Libraries**
    - Python's standard library and third-party packages (e.g., NumPy for numerical computations, SciPy for scientific calculations, OpenCV for computer vision, and TensorFlow or PyTorch for machine learning) offer powerful tools for data processing and algorithm development.
3. **Rapid Prototyping**
    - In robotics, you often need to test ideas quickly. Python's interpreted nature allows for fast iteration without the need for lengthy compile times.

4. **Vibrant Community**
    - Python boasts one of the largest developer communities in the world. This means a wealth of tutorials, Q&A forums, and open-source projects to build upon.
5. **Integration with ROS2**
    - ROS2 provides **rclpy**, the Python client library that lets you write nodes, services, and actions in Python. This tight integration means you can leverage Python's simplicity while interacting seamlessly with other ROS2 components.

1.3.2 Python vs. C++ in ROS2

While C++ is also a popular language in robotics—particularly for performance-critical parts—Python is ideal for rapid development and higher-level tasks such as:

- **Prototyping new algorithms**
- **Data analysis** (sensor data processing, machine learning)
- **Scripting repetitive tasks** (automating calibration or testing procedures)

For real-time operations and embedded systems with tight performance constraints, C++ might be the better choice. However, in many cases, you can combine **C++ and Python** in a single system, using C++ for critical components and

Python for everything else. This hybrid approach is not only viable but common in advanced robotics.

1.3.3 Example: Python in Action

Consider a scenario where you have a mobile robot equipped with a LiDAR and a camera. You might use **C++** for the LiDAR driver (ensuring high-frequency data capture), but **Python** for:

1. **Computer Vision:** Processing camera data via OpenCV to detect obstacles or recognize markers.
2. **SLAM (Simultaneous Localization and Mapping):** Running a Python-based SLAM library that merges LiDAR and vision data.
3. **High-Level Decision Making:** A Python node to handle logic and transitions between different robot modes (e.g., exploring, following a path, or stopping).

This blend leverages Python's simplicity for "thinking" and C++'s efficiency for "sensing" and "acting."

Diagram 1.3: Python-C++ Hybrid Architecture

```
+---------+                +---------+
| LiDAR   |---- C++ Node --->|         |
| Driver  |                |  ROS2   |--- Python Node -> High-Level Decision
+---------+                | Network |
                           +---------+

+---------+                +---------+
| Camera  |---- Python Node->|         |
| Driver  |                |         |
+---------+                +---------+
```

This diagram underscores how Python and C++ can coexist smoothly within a ROS2 network, each handling tasks best suited to its strengths.

1.3.4 Best Practices for Using Python in ROS2

1. **Keep It Modular**: Break down your code into small, reusable modules. This not only makes debugging easier but also lets you swap out components as needed.
2. **Use Virtual Environments**: Tools like venv or conda allow you to manage different versions of Python libraries for various projects without conflicts.
3. **Follow ROS2 Conventions**: Adhere to standard package naming, file structures, and coding styles to maintain clarity and consistency.
4. **Profile Your Code**: For performance-critical sections, use profiling tools (cProfile, line_profiler) to identify bottlenecks. If needed, move that part to C++.

Keep these pointers in mind, and you'll find Python to be an **indispensable ally** in your robotics journey.

1.4. Real-World Applications and Future Trends

Now that you understand **why** robotics matters today, what ROS2 is, and how Python plays into the equation, let's paint a bigger picture. **Where do all these technologies lead?** And **what kind of groundbreaking work is happening right now that you can be a part of?**

1.4.1 Current Real-World Applications

1. **Manufacturing and Warehousing**
   - **Robotic Arms:** Automated assembly lines, capable of operating around the clock to boost production.
   - **Autonomous Guided Vehicles (AGVs):** Move materials across large warehouses, optimizing logistics and reducing manual labor.
   - **Quality Control:** Vision-based inspection systems identify defective products at high speed.
2. **Healthcare**
   - **Surgical Robots:** Assist surgeons in performing delicate procedures with enhanced precision.
   - **Rehabilitation Devices:** Exoskeletons for patients recovering from injuries or coping with mobility issues.

- **Service Robots**: Sanitation and delivery robots in hospitals, reducing infection risks and assisting overworked staff.

3. **Agriculture**
   - **Crop Monitoring:** Drones equipped with multispectral cameras for analyzing crop health and yield forecasts.
   - **Automated Harvesters:** Robots that pick fruits or vegetables selectively, reducing labor shortages.
4. **Transportation**
   - **Self-Driving Cars**: Advanced driver-assistance systems that leverage LiDAR, radar, and cameras to navigate roads.
   - **Delivery Robots and Drones**: Last-mile delivery solutions that bring packages directly to consumers.
5. **Search and Rescue**
   - **Disaster Response Robots**: Navigate hazardous environments like collapsed buildings, detect survivors, and relay information back to rescue teams.
6. **Space Exploration**

- **Planetary Rovers**: Conduct scientific experiments on distant planets, collecting soil samples and sending data back to Earth.
- **Satellite Servicing Robots**: Perform maintenance and refueling tasks on orbiting satellites, extending their operational lifetimes.

1.4.2 Emerging Trends in Robotics

1. **Artificial Intelligence and Machine Learning**
   - **Reinforcement Learning**: Robots learning to optimize their behaviors through trial and error.
   - **Deep Learning**: Advanced neural networks for more accurate perception and decision-making.
2. **Edge and Cloud Robotics**
   - **Distributed Computing**: Splitting computation between the robot (edge) and powerful remote servers (cloud) for complex tasks.
   - **Autonomy at Scale**: With 5G connectivity, fleets of robots can coordinate in real-time over large areas.
3. **Human-Robot Collaboration**
   - **Cobots (Collaborative Robots)**: Designed to work side-by-side with humans, enhancing productivity without compromising safety.

- **Natural Language Interfaces:** Speech-based control to make interaction more intuitive.

4. **Nano Robotics**
    - While still in early stages, micro- or nano-scale robots hold potential for breakthroughs in targeted drug delivery or microsurgery.
5. **Sustainability and Environmental Robotics**
    - **Green Robotics:** Drones that monitor deforestation, ocean-cleaning robots, and devices that track wildlife to preserve biodiversity.

1.4.3 The Road Ahead

Robotics is a **transformative technology**, reshaping industries and opening up entirely new possibilities. As sensors become cheaper, AI algorithms become smarter, and connectivity improves, we can expect robots to be:

- **More Socially Integrated:** Serving as companions, assistants, or even household helpers.
- **Highly Specialized:** Tailored robots addressing niche tasks (e.g., tunnel inspection, underwater welding).
- **Increasingly Autonomous:** Minimizing human intervention for extended operations (like interplanetary missions).

Reflect on this: *Do you see yourself creating a robot that changes the way people live or work? Or contributing to open-source libraries that power the next era of automation? The choices are vast, and the tools—ROS2 and Python—are here to help you innovate.*

1.5. Book Structure and How to Use This Guide

To **maximize your learning experience**, it's important to understand how this book is organized. Each chapter addresses a specific aspect of robotic development using ROS2 and Python. While you can read it straight through, you may also pick and choose chapters based on your immediate needs and interests.

1.5.1 Chapter Breakdown

1. **Introduction to ROS2 and Python** (This Chapter)
    - You're currently here, getting the foundational context for robotics, ROS2, and Python. By now, you should have a sense of why these technologies are important.
2. **Setting Up Your Robotics Development Environment**
    - Step-by-step guidance on installing ROS2, configuring Python environments, managing

dependencies, and using essential command-line tools.

  - Ideal for beginners setting up a fresh workspace or professionals seeking a reliable environment.

3. **ROS2 Basics: Understanding the Core Concepts**
   - Deeper exploration of nodes, topics, services, actions, and how to structure your code in ROS2.
   - Crucial for building the mental models that will help you navigate more complex projects.
4. **Python Essentials for Robotics**
   - Covers Python syntax, best practices, libraries like NumPy and OpenCV, and how they apply to robotics tasks.
   - Even experienced Python developers can benefit from the robotics-specific examples and tips.
5. **Robot Architecture and Hardware Fundamentals**
   - Delves into the physical side of robotics: sensors, actuators, microcontrollers, and how to interface them with ROS2.
   - Includes practical wiring diagrams, best practices, and step-by-step instructions for bringing your hardware to life.

6. **Sensors and Perception**
   - Focuses on sensor fusion, vision processing, and how to integrate multiple data streams to give your robot a richer understanding of its surroundings.
7. **Robot Navigation and Path Planning**
   - Explains how to enable your robot to move through the world autonomously. SLAM (Simultaneous Localization and Mapping) and Nav2 (the ROS2 Navigation Stack) are key topics.
8. **State Machines and Behavior Trees**
   - Learn to manage complex robot behaviors systematically, allowing your robot to handle real-world unpredictability and gracefully recover from errors.
9. **Advanced Topics in ROS2 and Python**
   - Explores performance optimization, Docker deployments, real-time considerations, and more for those wanting to push the boundaries.
10. **Practical Applications and Case Studies**
    - Detailed examples of how robots are used in different industries (manufacturing, healthcare, space exploration), with real-world success stories and challenges.

11. **Building a Complete Robot from Scratch**
    - Combines mechanical design, software architecture, sensor integration, and testing into one cohesive project, reinforcing everything learned so far.
12. **Troubleshooting and Maintenance**
    - A compendium of common issues, diagnostic strategies, best practices for upkeep, and how to iteratively improve your robotic system.
13. **The Road Ahead**
    - Covers future trends, community involvement, research opportunities, and ongoing developments in ROS2, Python, and robotics in general.
14. **Appendices**
    - Quick references, glossaries, and additional resources to help you resolve issues quickly or explore advanced topics.

1.5.2 How to Navigate the Book

- **Linear Approach**: If you're brand new to robotics, consider reading from front to back. Chapters are arranged in a logical progression that builds upon previous ones.

- **Modular Approach:** If you already have a grasp of certain topics, jump to the chapters you find most relevant (e.g., navigation, sensors, or hardware interfacing).
- **Project-Focused:** Each chapter includes a hands-on project. If you're eager to start building immediately, look for these project sections to get practical experience as you read.

1.5.3 Tips for Getting the Most Out of Each Chapter

1. **Hands-On Exercises:** Don't just read—apply. Robotics is best learned by doing.
2. **Experiment:** Feel free to modify and adapt the sample code.
3. **Ask Questions:** Use online forums like ROS Discourse or Stack Overflow if you get stuck.
4. **Document Your Progress:** Keep notes of what worked, what didn't, and ideas for improvement.
5. **Collaborate:** Engage with local robotics clubs, online communities, or hackathons to share knowledge and accelerate learning.

1.5.4 A Quick Word on Versions

ROS2 has multiple distributions (e.g., Foxy, Galactic, Humble, Iron), each with specific release timelines and support windows. Python also has different versions, though Python 3.8+ is commonly recommended for modern development. In this book, we focus on **widely adopted, stable versions** of ROS2 and Python, but the core principles remain the same regardless of minor version differences. Always check official documentation and release notes if you're working with a newer or older version.

Conclusion of Chapter 1

In this opening chapter, we've explored **why robotics is booming, what ROS2 brings to the table, the role of Python in robot development**, and **where these technologies are being used in the real world**. We also provided a **roadmap** for navigating the rest of this book, ensuring you know where to find the resources and guidance you need.

Key Takeaways:

- **Why Robotics?** Rapid advancements in hardware, software, and community support make this the perfect time to dive into robotics.
- **ROS2 Overview:** ROS2 is a versatile, next-generation middleware that excels in modularity, multi-platform

support, and real-time communication, making it well-suited for both hobby and industrial-grade robots.

- **Python's Power**: Python speeds up development thanks to its simplicity, large ecosystem of libraries, and vibrant community. It is a perfect fit for high-level robotics tasks while coexisting seamlessly with C++ where performance is critical.
- **Real-World Impact**: From automated warehouses to surgical units, robotics is changing industries and daily life. Understanding these applications helps frame the importance of ROS2 and Python skills.
- **Book Structure**: Each chapter drills into a specific domain (hardware, navigation, perception, advanced topics) and includes hands-on projects. Leverage this modular layout to focus on the areas that interest you the most.

By continuing through the book, you'll gain **practical experience** in setting up a ROS2 development environment, writing Python nodes, integrating hardware, and even building a complete robot from scratch. We'll tackle everything from the simplest sensor reading to advanced navigation, ensuring you have the skills to innovate and explore new horizons in robotics.

Chapter 2: Setting Up Your Robotics Development Environment

Welcome to your next step in building intelligent robots that can sense, navigate, and solve real-world problems! If Chapter 1 provided a bird's-eye view of why robotics is so crucial today—and how ROS2 and Python fit into the grand scheme of things—this chapter is all about **getting your hands dirty** with the nuts and bolts of a reliable, robust development environment. From choosing the right hardware to installing ROS2 on different operating systems, we're going to walk through everything you need to hit the ground running.

By the end of this chapter, you'll have a fully functioning robotics environment—tailored to your platform of choice—alongside an understanding of core command-line tools, Python libraries, and best practices for version control. Ready? Let's dive in!

2.1. Hardware and Software Requirements

Before you delve into code, it's vital to ensure your **hardware** (physical components and computing devices) and **software** (operating systems, drivers, libraries) meet the requirements for developing and running ROS2-based robotics applications. Think of it like preparing a kitchen before you bake a cake: you need the right utensils, ingredients, and the right oven settings!

2.1.1. Choosing Your Main Computing Platform

Which machine should you use to develop robotics projects? Short answer: whichever meets these essential criteria:

1. **Processing Power**:
   - ROS2 can run on a variety of hardware, from laptops and desktops to single-board computers (SBCs) like the Raspberry Pi.
   - For **simulation or resource-heavy tasks** (e.g., computer vision, path planning, machine learning), you'll want at least an Intel i5 (or AMD equivalent) processor, 8 GB of RAM, and a decent graphics card (or integrated GPU).
   - For **lightweight or embedded tasks**, a Raspberry Pi 4 (4 GB RAM) or NVIDIA Jetson Nano can suffice—especially if you plan to move your code onto a physical robot later.
2. **Operating System Compatibility**:

- ROS2 supports **Ubuntu**, **Windows**, and **macOS**. However, **Ubuntu** (LTS versions like 20.04, 22.04) is the most popular and well-documented environment.
- If you're on Windows or macOS, rest assured you can still follow along; just be mindful of slight differences in commands and installation processes.

3. **Storage Space:**
   - Ensure you have **at least 20 GB** free for the operating system, ROS2 installation, and additional libraries. If you plan on storing large datasets (common in robotics), aim for more—around 100 GB or higher.
4. **Connectivity:**
   - ROS2 relies heavily on network communication between nodes (processes). If you plan on distributed robotics—where multiple devices communicate wirelessly—you'll need a **stable Wi-Fi** or Ethernet connection.

2.1.2. Considerations for Robot-Specific Hardware

If you're planning on **physical** robotics (rather than just simulations), you'll also need to factor in these devices:

1. **Microcontrollers and SBCs:** Arduino, Teensy, or Raspberry Pi can handle sensor data and direct control of motors.
2. **Sensors:** LiDAR, IMU (Inertial Measurement Unit), camera modules, ultrasonic sensors, or GPS—depending on your project's objectives.
3. **Actuators:** DC motors, stepper motors, servo motors, or robotic arms that will perform tasks in the physical world.
4. **Motor Drivers / Controllers:** Bridges the gap between your microcontroller and the motors.
5. **Power Supply:** Batteries, voltage regulators, or power adapters that deliver stable current.
6. **Communication Modules:** If you're building drones or mobile robots, consider wireless communication (Wi-Fi, Bluetooth, or even LoRa for extended range).

Analogy: *Think of your robot as a human body. The main computing platform is the* ***brain****, microcontrollers are the* ***nerves****, sensors are the* ***eyes and ears****, and actuators are the* ***arms and legs****. Each part must function harmoniously.*

2.1.3. Software: Beyond the Operating System

Aside from your OS, be mindful of these **software must-haves:**

1. **ROS2 Distribution**: Select a stable distribution (e.g., Foxy, Galactic, Humble, Iron) with robust community support.
2. **Python 3.8 or Higher**: ROS2 packages often require Python 3.8 or later.
3. **CMake & Build Essentials**: Allows you to compile ROS2 packages from source, if needed.
4. **Development Environments**: Visual Studio Code, PyCharm, or even simple text editors like Nano and Vim.
5. **Git**: Essential for version control (we'll cover this in detail in section 2.5).

If your environment checks all the boxes above, you're ready to proceed. Don't worry if it feels like a lot—**start small, upgrade as needed**, and you'll be well on your way.

2.2. Installing ROS2: Step-by-Step (Ubuntu, Windows, macOS)

Installing ROS2 can initially feel daunting because it involves dependencies and environment variables. Fear not! We're going to walk through each operating system's setup. By the end, you'll have a functioning ROS2 installation suited for robotics development.

Important: *This guide references widely supported ROS2 distributions (like **Humble** or **Iron**). Installation steps are similar across distributions, but always check the official ROS2 documentation for the latest instructions if you're using a newer version.*

2.2.1 Installing ROS2 on Ubuntu

Ubuntu is widely considered the **gold standard** for ROS2 development due to its compatibility and community support. We'll assume you're on Ubuntu 22.04 (Jammy), but the steps for Ubuntu 20.04 (Focal) are similar.

2.2.1.1. Add the ROS2 Repository

1. **Update and Upgrade:**

```bash
sudo apt update
sudo apt upgrade
```

2. **Locale Setup:**

```bash
sudo locale-gen en_US en_US.UTF-8
sudo update-locale LC_ALL=en_US.UTF-8
LANG=en_US.UTF-8
```

3. **Add the ROS2 GPG Key:**

```bash
```

```
sudo apt install curl gnupg lsb-release
curl -sSL
https://raw.githubusercontent.com/ros/rosdistro/m
aster/ros.asc | sudo apt-key add -
```

4. **Add the ROS2 Repository:**

```
bash


sudo sh -c 'echo "deb [arch=$(dpkg --print-
architecture)]
http://packages.ros.org/ros2/ubuntu $(lsb_release
-cs) main" > /etc/apt/sources.list.d/ros2-
latest.list'
```

2.2.1.2. Install ROS2 Packages

1. **Update the Package Index:**

```
bash


sudo apt update
```

2. **Install the ROS2 Meta-Package:**

```
bash


sudo apt install ros-humble-desktop
```

Replace **humble** with **foxy**, **galactic**, or **iron** if you prefer a different distribution.

3. **ROS2 Environment Setup:**

```
bash
```

```
echo "source /opt/ros/humble/setup.bash" >>
~/.bashrc
source ~/.bashrc
```

This ensures that every new terminal automatically sources ROS2 environment variables.

4. **Verify Installation:**

```bash

printenv | grep -i ROS
```

You should see environment variables like ROS_VERSION, ROS_DISTRO, etc.

2.2.1.3. Creating a ROS2 Workspace

1. **Create a Directory:**

```bash

mkdir -p ~/ros2_ws/src
cd ~/ros2_ws
```

2. **Initialize a Workspace:**

```bash

colcon build
```

3. **Add the Workspace to Your Environment:**

```bash
```

```
source install/setup.bash
```

4. **Test:**

```bash
ros2 run demo_nodes_cpp talker
```

Open another terminal, source your ROS2 environment, and:

```bash
ros2 run demo_nodes_py listener
```

You should see "Hello World" messages in real-time.

ROS2 Workspace Structure

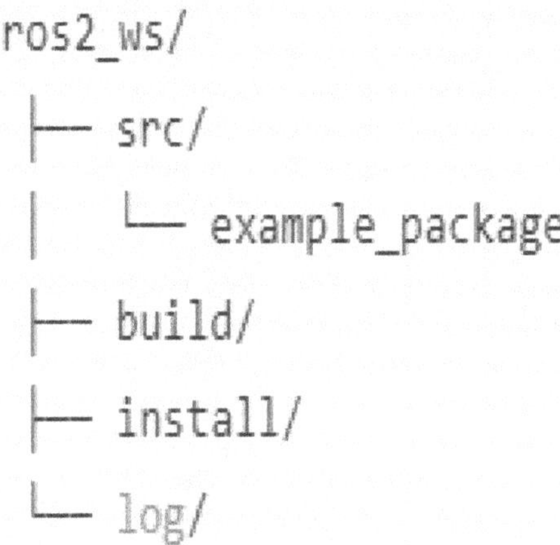

This diagram illustrates the typical structure of a ROS2 workspace, with src containing your packages, build holding compiled artifacts, and install containing executable files.

2.2.2 Installing ROS2 on Windows

Windows support for ROS2 has improved significantly. While Ubuntu remains more common, many users prefer Windows for familiarity or hardware constraints.

2.2.2.1. Install Dependencies

1. **Chocolatey:** If you don't have it, install Chocolatey:

```
powershell


Set-ExecutionPolicy AllSigned
Set-ExecutionPolicy Bypass -Scope Process
[System.Net.ServicePointManager]::SecurityProtoco
l =
[System.Net.ServicePointManager]::SecurityProtoco
l -bor 3072
iex ((New-Object
System.Net.WebClient).DownloadString('https://com
munity.chocolatey.org/install.ps1'))
```

2. **Visual Studio:** You need **Visual Studio 2019** or later with the Desktop development with C++ workload installed.

3. **Python 3.8 or Newer:** Download from python.org or install via Chocolatey:

```
powershell


choco install python --version=3.8.10
```

2.2.2.2. Install ROS2 Binaries

1. **Download the ROS2 Installer** from the official ROS2 Releases.
2. **Run the .exe** installer. Follow on-screen instructions, selecting typical installation.
3. **Add Environment Variables:**
    - You may need to manually add the bin folder of the ROS2 installation to your PATH.
    - For example: C:\dev\ros2_humble\bin.

2.2.2.3. Setup a ROS2 Workspace on Windows

1. **Open a Visual Studio Command Prompt** (x64 Native Tools).
2. **Create the Workspace:**

```
powershell

mkdir ros2_ws\src
cd ros2_ws
```

3. **Build:**

```
powershell

colcon build
```

4. **Source the Environment:**

```
powershell
```

```
call install/setup.bat
```

5. **Test:**

```powershell
ros2 run demo_nodes_cpp talker
```

In another prompt, run:

```powershell
ros2 run demo_nodes_py listener
```

Check if messages are flowing.

2.2.3 Installing ROS2 on macOS

While not as common as Ubuntu, **macOS** can still host ROS2 development quite well.

2.2.3.1. Install Homebrew

- If you haven't already, install Homebrew:

```bash
/bin/bash -c "$(curl -fsSL https://raw.githubusercontent.com/Homebrew/install/HEAD/install.sh)"
```

2.2.3.2. Dependencies via Homebrew

1. **Update Homebrew:**

```bash
brew update
```

2. **Install ROS2 Dependencies:**

```bash
brew install python cmake pkg-config openssl
```

You may also need additional packages depending on the ROS2 distribution.

2.2.3.3. Building ROS2 from Source on macOS

Currently, official macOS binaries for newer ROS2 distributions might be limited. In some cases, you'll build from source:

1. **Clone the ROS2 Repositories** into a workspace directory (e.g., ~/ros2_ws/src).
2. **Use colcon** to build.

```bash
cd ~/ros2_ws
colcon build --symlink-install
```

3. **Source:**

```bash
```

```
source install/setup.bash
```

4. **Test:**

```
bash

ros2 run demo_nodes_cpp talker
```

And in another terminal:

```
bash

ros2 run demo_nodes_py listener
```

2.2.4 Post-Installation Checks

Regardless of your operating system, it's vital to verify that **ROS2 commands** are available and your environment is correctly configured. A few quick checks:

- which ros2 or where ros2 (Windows) should point to the executable in the correct directory.
- colcon should be recognized as a command.
- printenv | grep ROS (or echo %ROS_DISTRO% in Windows) shows the distribution name.

Key Insight: *If something isn't working,* ***double-check*** *your environment variables, especially if you're using multiple terminals. You might need to source your workspace again or confirm your installation paths.*

2.3. Python Versions and Key Libraries for Robotics

ROS2 is language-agnostic, meaning you can use C++, Python, or other languages. However, Python remains a top choice for **rapid development**, **machine learning integration**, and **high-level scripting**.

2.3.1 Choosing the Right Python Version

Most modern ROS2 distributions expect **Python 3.8** or higher. Here's why:

1. **Long-Term Support**: Python 3.8+ versions typically receive security fixes and improvements.
2. **Library Compatibility**: Many robotics libraries are tested against 3.8 or above.
3. **Performance Enhancements**: Each new Python release brings minor speedups and new language features.

2.3.2 Using Virtual Environments

Keeping your Python dependencies isolated is crucial. Virtual environments let you maintain separate sets of libraries for different projects, reducing conflicts.

Creating a Virtual Environment (using venv):

```bash
python3 -m venv ~/venv/ros2
source ~/venv/ros2/bin/activate
```

Within this virtual environment, you can install project-specific Python packages without messing up your global system.

2.3.3 Must-Have Python Libraries for Robotics

1. **NumPy**: The backbone of numerical computations and array manipulations. Perfect for sensor data processing or matrix operations.

```bash
pip install numpy
```

2. **OpenCV-Python**: Essential for **computer vision tasks** such as object detection, image processing, or camera calibration.

```bash
pip install opencv-python
```

3. **SciPy**: Offers advanced math functions, optimizations, and signal processing routines. Great for analyzing sensor signals.

```bash
pip install scipy
```

4. **Matplotlib** or **Plotly**: Useful for **visualizing sensor data** and debugging algorithms.

```bash
pip install matplotlib
```

5. **Pandas**: While more common in data science, it's helpful if you need to handle large CSV files of sensor logs or time-series data.

```bash
pip install pandas
```

6. **TensorFlow or PyTorch**: If you're integrating deep learning (e.g., for object recognition or advanced path planning), consider installing one of these frameworks.

```bash
pip install tensorflow
# or
pip install torch
```

7. **rclpy**: The official Python client library for ROS2. Typically installed automatically with your ROS2 distribution, but you can re-install or upgrade if needed.

bash

pip install rclpy

8. **pytest:** For running automated tests on your robotics code, ensuring reliability.

bash

pip install pytest

Typical Python Ecosystem for Robotics

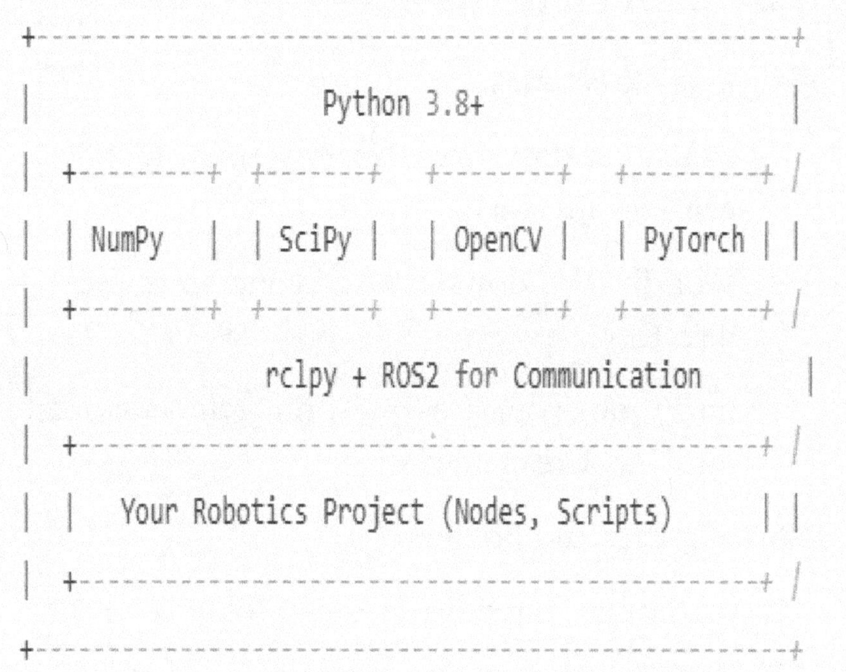

This diagram shows how your Python environment forms the core of your robotics stack, providing numerical, vision, and machine learning capabilities, all orchestrated by ROS2's messaging tools.

2.4. Essential Command Line Tools and ROS2 Command Overview

Command line interfaces (CLIs) might seem intimidating, but they offer speed, control, and automation power. In the robotics world—where you'll frequently switch between nodes, logs, and network configurations—**knowing your way around a terminal** is indispensable.

2.4.1 Command Line Basics

1. **Navigating Directories:**
    - cd path/to/directory changes your current working directory.
    - ls or dir (Windows) lists the contents of the directory.
    - pwd shows your present working directory path (on Unix-like systems).
2. **Managing Files and Folders:**
    - mkdir new_directory creates a folder.
    - rm filename (Unix) or del filename (Windows) removes a file.
    - cp, mv (Unix) or copy, move (Windows) to copy or move items.
3. **Using a Text Editor:**

    - Nano or Vim on Unix, Notepad++ or VS Code on Windows.

4. **System Monitoring:**
    - top, htop (Unix) for CPU/memory usage.
    - taskmgr or Resource Monitor on Windows.

2.4.2 ROS2 Command Line Tools

ROS2 includes **built-in** command line tools to help you interact with nodes, topics, and more.

1. **Listing Nodes:**

```
bash

ros2 node list
```

    - Shows all active nodes in your ROS2 network.

2. **Showing Node Info:**

```
bash

ros2 node info /node_name
```

    - Reveals the topics a node publishes or subscribes to, along with any services or parameters.

3. **Listing Topics:**

```
bash

ros2 topic list
```

- Enumerates all published and subscribed topics.

4. **Echo a Topic:**

```
bash

ros2 topic echo /topic_name
```

- Streams live data from that topic to your terminal.

5. **Publish to a Topic:**

```
bash

ros2 topic pub /topic_name std_msgs/msg/String
"data: 'Hello Robot!'"
```

- Sends a test message to a topic, which can be useful for debugging.

6. **Service Call:**

```
bash

ros2 service call /service_name
std_srvs/srv/Empty "{}"
```

- Invokes a service with the relevant request data.

7. **Launch Files:**

```
bash

ros2 launch package_name launch_file.launch.py
```

  - Starts multiple nodes as configured in a launch file, which is incredibly helpful for complex systems.

8. **Parameter Management:**

```
bash


ros2 param list
ros2 param get /node_name parameter_name
ros2 param set /node_name parameter_name
new_value
```

  - Allows real-time adjustments to a node's configuration without recompiling code.

2.4.3 Colcon: Building and Bundling Packages

While colcon is not strictly a ROS2 command (it's a standalone build tool), it's integral to the ROS2 workflow:

- **colcon build**: Compiles your packages.
- **colcon test:** Runs any tests you've defined.
- **colcon build –symlink-install:** Useful for Python packages, letting you edit code without repeatedly re-installing.

2.5. Version Control with Git: Keeping Your Projects Organized

Imagine working on a robotics codebase with multiple collaborators. Someone updates the navigation logic, someone else tweaks sensor calibration, and you also have your own local changes. Without a robust **version control system**, chaos ensues. Enter **Git**.

2.5.1 Why Git Matters in Robotics

1. **Collaboration:** Git enables multiple people to work on the same project simultaneously, merging changes in an orderly fashion.
2. **Track Changes:** You can revert to a stable state if something breaks, saving you from hours of debugging.
3. **Branching and Merging:** Develop features in isolation, merge only when stable. Ideal for experimental robotics modules.
4. **Open-Source Integration:** If you plan to share or fork open-source robotics packages, Git is the standard.

2.5.2 Basic Git Workflow

1. **Initialize a Repository:**

```
bash

cd ~/ros2_ws
```

```
git init
```

This creates a .git folder for version tracking.

2. **Create a .gitignore:**
    - Typically you ignore build artifacts like build/, install/, or log/. Add a .gitignore file in the root of your workspace:

```bash
build/
install/
log/
.DS_Store
*.pyc
```

    - This keeps your repo clean and free of unnecessary files.

3. **Stage and Commit:**

```bash
git add .
git commit -m "Initial commit"
```

This snapshots your current code state.

4. **Branching:**

```bash
git checkout -b feature/my_new_feature
```

Develop your new feature on this branch.

5. **Merging:**

```bash
git checkout main
git merge feature/my_new_feature
```

Incorporates your feature into the main branch once it's tested and stable.

6. **Pushing to Remote:**

```bash
git remote add origin
https://github.com/YourUsername/YourRepo.git
git push -u origin main
```

This puts your code on a remote repository like GitHub or GitLab, enabling backups and collaboration.

2.5.3 Best Practices for Robotics Projects

1. **Use Descriptive Commit Messages:** Instead of "Fix stuff," say "Fix odometry calculation for differential drive." This helps future you understand what changed.

2. **Branch per Feature:** Keep your main branch as stable as possible.

3. **Frequent Commits**: Commit as soon as you have a small, logical chunk of work done.
4. **Pull Requests and Reviews**: If you're on a team, create **pull requests** and ask for reviews before merging major changes.
5. **Tagging and Releases**: When your robot hits a milestone—like a working prototype—tag that commit so you can easily reference it later.

Putting It All Together

Congratulations! You've now explored:

- **2.1 Hardware and Software Requirements**: What machine, components, and OS you'll need.
- **2.2 Installing ROS2: Step-by-Step** for Ubuntu, Windows, and macOS. Each step ensures you have a working environment.
- **2.3 Python Versions and Key Libraries**: Why Python 3.8+ is recommended and which libraries you'll lean on most in robotics.
- **2.4 Essential Command Line Tools and ROS2 Command Overview**: The bread-and-butter commands that let you manage nodes, topics, and more.

- **2.5 Version Control with Git:** How to keep your projects organized and collaborate effectively.

At this point, you have the infrastructure in place to build and manage a ROS2 application, whether it's purely software-based or extends to physical robots. If you followed the step-by-step instructions, you should have **ROS2 installed**, a **Python environment** configured, **Git** initialized for version control, and a fundamental grasp of how to navigate the command line. This sets the stage for deeper dives into **robot architecture**, **sensor integration**, and more advanced robotics concepts that will follow in later chapters.

Summary of Key Learnings

1. **Plan Your Hardware Wisely:** You don't need the biggest, baddest system, but it helps to have enough CPU/RAM if you're doing heavy simulations or advanced AI.
2. **ROS2 Installation:** The process varies slightly by platform, but the core concepts—adding repositories, installing packages, sourcing your environment—remain the same.
3. **Python 3.8+ is King:** Libraries like NumPy, OpenCV, and TensorFlow are essential for any cutting-edge robotics project.
4. **CLI Mastery:** Knowing ros2 topic, ros2 node, and colcon build commands inside and out will streamline your workflow.

5. **Git**: Version control is not optional—it's your lifeline when something goes wrong or multiple collaborators are involved.

Frequently Asked Questions (FAQ)

Q1: I installed ROS2 on Ubuntu, but ros2 command not found keeps appearing. What should I do?
A1: Make sure you've sourced your ROS2 setup script in your ~/.bashrc. For example:

```bash
echo "source /opt/ros/humble/setup.bash" >>
~/.bashrc
source ~/.bashrc
```

Also confirm you're in a fresh terminal session where those variables are loaded.

Q2: Which distribution should I choose—Foxy, Galactic, Humble, or Iron?
A2: Typically, choose the latest **LTS** (Long-Term Support) distribution for long-term stability. If you need cutting-edge features, you may opt for the most recent release—just be aware that it might not be as thoroughly tested.

Q3: Why do I need a separate ROS2 workspace (ros2_ws) instead of just coding in my home directory?
A3: A workspace keeps your project organized, letting you build, install, and log all in a structured environment. It also simplifies colcon usage.

Q4: Do I really need Git if I'm a solo developer?
A4: Absolutely. Even if you're alone, Git provides version history, rollback points, and an easy way to maintain backups. You'll thank yourself later.

Q5: My installation took up more space than expected. How can I reduce the footprint?
A5: You can remove **debug** symbol packages, do partial installs instead of the full desktop meta-package, or rely on containerization (like Docker) to manage dependencies.

What's Next?

With your development environment set up, the next chapter will guide you through the **core concepts of ROS2**—nodes, topics, services, actions—and how to structure your robot software. This foundational knowledge will be crucial as we progress to **sensors**, **navigation**, and eventually **building a complete robot**.

Remember: robotics is a **hands-on** domain. If you run into errors, try to **troubleshoot** methodically:

- Double-check environment variables.
- Look for missing dependencies or incorrectly typed commands.
- Consult community forums like ROS Discourse or relevant GitHub issues.

And, of course, **don't be afraid to experiment.** The beauty of open-source robotics is that you have the freedom to explore, break things, and fix them again—each time learning something new. So give yourself permission to tinker, and enjoy the journey!

Chapter 3: ROS2 Basics—Understanding the Core Concepts

Robotics is complex because it involves orchestrating multiple systems to perform tasks in real-time. Yet, the beauty of **ROS2** (Robot Operating System 2) lies in how it abstracts away much of that complexity, allowing you to focus on **functionality** rather than low-level plumbing. In this chapter, we'll take a deep dive into the foundation of ROS2: **Nodes, Topics, Services, and Actions**, how **message passing** works, and how to organize your code using **launch files** and **packages**. We'll also walk through **real-world examples**–including a hands-on project called **"Hello, Robot!"**–so you can see these concepts in action. By the end of this chapter, you'll have a solid understanding of the building blocks that make ROS2 such a powerful tool for robotics development.

Important Note: We'll keep things **simple, jargon-free**, and break down each concept into **actionable steps** with diagrams and code snippets, ensuring you gain a **practical**, intuitive grasp of ROS2 fundamentals without repeating material from previous chapters.

3.1. Nodes, Topics, Services, and Actions

If you think of a robot as a team, then each **team member** has a specific role. One may gather sensor data, another handles motor control, yet another may process camera images. In ROS2, each of these "team members" is known as a **node**. But how do these nodes communicate? They use **topics, services, and actions**, forming the communication backbone of a ROS2 system.

3.1.1 Nodes: Modular Building Blocks

A **node** is simply an executable (a process) in ROS2 that performs a well-defined task or set of tasks. Here are some **key advantages** of breaking a robot's software into multiple nodes:

1. **Modularity:** If one node crashes, the others can keep running, making the entire system more robust.
2. **Reusability:** A node designed for reading a sensor in one project can be reused in another, as long as the sensor is the same type.
3. **Distributed Processing:** Nodes can run on different machines (or microcontrollers) in a network, useful if your robot has multiple onboard computers or an external server for heavy computation.

Analogy: *Think of a node as a single app on your smartphone. Each app (node) is focused on one function—like reading a sensor or controlling a motor.*

3.1.2 Topics: Sharing Streams of Data

Topics are **named communication channels** used by nodes to exchange data in a **publish-subscribe** fashion.

- **Publishers:** Nodes that send data (e.g., a sensor node might publish temperature readings).
- **Subscribers:** Nodes that receive data (e.g., a monitoring node that logs these readings to a file).

Crucially, **publishers** and **subscribers** don't need to know about each other. As long as they use the same topic name and compatible message type, data will flow seamlessly.

Advantages:

1. **Decoupled Communication:** Nodes can be developed and tested independently.
2. **Flexible:** Multiple nodes can subscribe to the same topic, or a single node can subscribe to many topics.

Example usage:

- A robot's **LiDAR** node publishes distance scans on a topic named /scan.
- A **navigation** node subscribes to /scan so it can avoid obstacles.

3.1.3 Services: Request-Response Interactions

While topics are good for streaming data, certain tasks require a **synchronous interaction**—a node needs to request something and get a direct response. That's where **services** shine.

- **Service Server:** A node that advertises a service (like "Please calculate the sum of two numbers").
- **Service Client:** A node that calls this service (it sends the two numbers and waits for the result).

Real-World Analogy: *Services are like calling a function in regular programming—when you call it, you wait until you get a reply. Topics, on the other hand, are more like radio broadcasts; they keep sending messages whether anyone's listening or not.*

3.1.4 Actions: Long-Running Tasks with Feedback

Some tasks are neither simple data streams nor quick request-responses. Instead, they take a while to complete, and you want **progress updates** or the ability to **cancel** if something goes wrong. This is where **actions** come in.

Example scenarios:

- **Navigation:** Sending a robot to a specific location is not instantaneous. You'll want feedback on whether it's on its way, how close it is, and if you need to cancel mid-route.

- **Pick-and-Place**: Involves multiple sub-steps—moving a robotic arm, gripping an object, placing it elsewhere—and can take several seconds to minutes.

Actions work by using a **goal** request, a feedback stream for updates, and a **result** message when the task completes (or fails).

3.2. Message Passing and Data Structures in ROS2

With nodes now in place, how do they pass data around? Let's talk about **message passing**—the heart of ROS2—and the **data structures** (also called message types) used to convey information.

3.2.1. Under the Hood: DDS and ROS2

ROS2 uses **DDS (Data Distribution Service)** under the covers. Although knowing all the DDS internals isn't strictly necessary for day-to-day usage, understanding that DDS handles discovery, quality of service (QoS), and data transport is useful. Essentially, when you run multiple nodes, **DDS** automatically helps them **discover** each other in the network, facilitating data exchange via topics, services, and actions.

3.2.2. Message Types

Messages in ROS2 are strongly typed. For instance, if a node publishes data of type std_msgs/msg/String, subscribers expecting that exact type can receive it. Common message types include:

1. **std_msgs/msg/String**: For text messages (logging, debugging, user input).
2. **std_msgs/msg/Float32**: For single floating-point values (temperature, CPU usage).
3. **geometry_msgs/msg/Twist**: Holds linear and angular velocities, often used for controlling a mobile robot's movement.
4. **sensor_msgs/msg/Image**: Represents camera frames or images.
5. **sensor_msgs/msg/LaserScan**: Used with LiDAR to convey distance readings in an arc around the robot.
6. **nav_msgs/msg/Odometry**: Conveys position, velocity, and orientation data—critical for navigation.

Creating Your Own Message Types: If existing message types don't suit your needs, you can define custom messages by adding .msg files in a package. You'll specify the fields (e.g., float32 x, float32 y) just like struct definitions in C. ROS2 automatically generates the necessary code for you to use them in Python, C++, or other supported languages.

3.2.3. Quality of Service (QoS)

One of the big improvements in ROS2 is fine-grained QoS settings, controlling:

- **Reliability:** Do you want best-effort message delivery (okay to drop some messages) or reliable delivery (like TCP)?
- **Durability:** Should new subscribers receive a queue of old messages, or only new ones?
- **Deadline:** How often must messages be delivered?

For most casual projects, **default QoS** is adequate. But in real-time or industrial settings, you may need to customize QoS for guaranteed performance.

3.2.4. How Nodes Exchange Data (Step-by-Step)

Let's walk through an example:

1. **Publisher Node** (e.g., a sensor node) advertises it will publish sensor_msgs/msg/LaserScan on /scan.
2. **Subscriber Node** (e.g., a mapping algorithm) subscribes to the topic /scan, expecting messages of the same type.
3. **DDS Discovery:** The two nodes find each other automatically if they share the same ROS2 domain and QoS settings.

4. **Data Flow:** The sensor node sends out messages at a set frequency (say 10 Hz), and the subscriber node receives them for processing.

Basic Publish-Subscribe Architecture

```
Publisher (Sensor Node)  -->  /scan  -->  Subscriber (Mapping Node)
          |                                      ^
          |                                      |
          +----->  DDS Discovery  <-----+
```

Above, you see the high-level flow where DDS is abstracted away, yet it manages under-the-hood networking.

3.3. Launch Files and Packages: Organizing Your Robot's Software

As robotics projects grow, you'll juggle dozens of nodes, custom messages, and dependencies. This section explains how **ROS2 packages** and **launch files** keep everything neat and maintainable.

3.3.1. Packages in ROS2

A **package** in ROS2 is essentially a folder containing related software, such as:

- **Source code** (Python or C++ nodes)
- **Message definitions** (if you're defining custom messages or services)
- **Launch files**
- **Configuration files**
- **Package metadata** (like package.xml and setup.py)

You can think of a package as a **container** for everything needed to execute a specific function, such as **lidar_reader**, **arm_controller**, or **image_processing.**

3.3.1.1. Creating a Package

Let's see a **step-by-step** approach to creating a simple Python package named my_robot_package:

1. **Navigate to your Workspace:**

```
bash


cd ~/ros2_ws/src
```

2. **Use ROS2 CLI:**

```
bash


ros2 pkg create my_robot_package --build-type
ament_python
```

This automatically generates a package structure:

```
arduino

my_robot_package/
 ├── package.xml
 ├── setup.py
 └── my_robot_package
      └── __init__.py
```

3. **Add Python Scripts**: Inside my_robot_package/my_robot_package, you can create Python nodes (e.g., publisher_node.py).
4. **Update package.xml**: Add dependencies, authors, maintainers, and descriptions.
5. **Build**:

```
bash

cd ~/ros2_ws
colcon build
source install/setup.bash
```

6. **Run**:

```
bash

ros2 run my_robot_package publisher_node
```

(Assuming publisher_node is a Python script with an entry point defined in setup.py.)

3.3.2. Launch Files

For small demos, running each node manually with ros2 run ... is fine. But as soon as you have multiple nodes to start at once—or you need specific parameter configurations—**launch files** become critical.

Launch files in ROS2 are typically Python scripts (.launch.py) that specify:

- Which nodes to launch
- Arguments or parameters for each node
- Event handlers (e.g., what to do if a node crashes)
- Namespaces for grouping nodes logically

3.3.2.1. Example Launch File

Below is a sample launch file named my_robot_launch.launch.py:

```python

from launch import LaunchDescription
from launch_ros.actions import Node

def generate_launch_description():
    return LaunchDescription([
        Node(
            package='my_robot_package',
            executable='publisher_node',
            name='publisher',
```

```
            output='screen'
        ),
        Node(
            package='my_robot_package',
            executable='subscriber_node',
            name='subscriber',
            output='screen'
        ),
    ])
```

Explanation:

1. We import LaunchDescription and Node from the launch_ros package.
2. The generate_launch_description() function returns a LaunchDescription object containing two nodes: publisher_node and subscriber_node.
3. Each Node is configured with a specific package, executable, and some settings (like whether to show output in the terminal).

To run this launch file:

```
bash

ros2 launch my_robot_package
my_robot_launch.launch.py
```

Both nodes will spring to life simultaneously.

3.4. Real-World Example: Building a Simple Publisher/Subscriber in Python

The best way to grasp these fundamentals is to see them in action. Let's build a straightforward **publisher** that sends out a text string on a topic, and a **subscriber** that listens to it.

3.4.1. Step-by-Step Setup

1. **Create a Package**
   Navigate to your workspace's src folder:

```bash
cd ~/ros2_ws/src
ros2 pkg create ros2_publisher_subscriber --
build-type ament_python
```

A new folder, ros2_publisher_subscriber, is generated with the necessary boilerplate.

2. **Folder Structure**
   Inside ros2_publisher_subscriber/ros2_publisher_subscriber, create two Python scripts:
   - simple_publisher.py
   - simple_subscriber.py
3. **Edit simple_publisher.py**

```python
python

#!/usr/bin/env python3

import rclpy
from rclpy.node import Node
from std_msgs.msg import String

class SimplePublisher(Node):
    def __init__(self):
        super().__init__('simple_publisher')
        self.publisher_ =
self.create_publisher(String, 'chatter', 10)
        timer_period = 1.0  # seconds
        self.timer =
self.create_timer(timer_period,
self.timer_callback)
        self.count = 0

    def timer_callback(self):
        msg = String()
        msg.data = f"Hello from ROS2, count:
{self.count}"
        self.publisher_.publish(msg)
        self.get_logger().info(f"Publishing:
{msg.data}")
        self.count += 1
```

```
def main(args=None):
    rclpy.init(args=args)
    node = SimplePublisher()
    rclpy.spin(node)
    node.destroy_node()
    rclpy.shutdown()

if __name__ == '__main__':
    main()
```

Explanation:

- **Line 1**: Shebang for Python 3.
- **Imports**: rclpy for ROS2 in Python, Node as the node base class, and String for the message type.
- **class SimplePublisher**:
  - Inherits from Node, naming itself 'simple_publisher'.
  - Creates a publisher for String messages on the topic **chatter** with a queue size of **10**.
  - Sets up a timer that calls timer_callback every second.
  - timer_callback constructs a String message, logs it, and publishes it on chatter.

4. **Edit simple_subscriber.py**

python

```
#!/usr/bin/env python3

import rclpy
from rclpy.node import Node
from std_msgs.msg import String

class SimpleSubscriber(Node):
    def __init__(self):
        super().__init__('simple_subscriber')
        self.subscription =
self.create_subscription(
            String,
            'chatter',
            self.listener_callback,
            10
        )
        self.subscription  # prevent unused
variable warning

    def listener_callback(self, msg):
        self.get_logger().info(f"I heard:
{msg.data}")

def main(args=None):
    rclpy.init(args=args)
    node = SimpleSubscriber()
    rclpy.spin(node)
```

```
    node.destroy_node()
    rclpy.shutdown()

if __name__ == '__main__':
    main()
```

Explanation:

- **class SimpleSubscriber:**
    - Subscribes to the same chatter topic.
    - Each time a message arrives, listener_callback is triggered, logging the received string.

5. **Modify setup.py** (in ros2_publisher_subscriber/):

```
python

from setuptools import setup

package_name = 'ros2_publisher_subscriber'

setup(
    name=package_name,
    version='0.0.0',
    packages=[package_name],
    data_files=[

('share/ament_index/resource_index/packages',
            ['resource/' + package_name]),
```

```
        ('share/' + package_name,
['package.xml']),
    ],
    install_requires=['setuptools'],
    zip_safe=True,
    maintainer='YourName',
    maintainer_email='YourEmail@example.com',
    description='Example ROS2 pub-sub in Python',
    license='Apache License 2.0',
    tests_require=['pytest'],
    entry_points={
        'console_scripts': [
            'simple_publisher =
ros2_publisher_subscriber.simple_publisher:main',
            'simple_subscriber =
ros2_publisher_subscriber.simple_subscriber:main'
,
        ],
    },
)
```

This **entry_points** section ensures we can run simple_publisher and simple_subscriber using ros2 run.

6. **Build and Source:**

```
bash

cd ~/ros2_ws
colcon build
```

```
source install/setup.bash
```

7. **Test:**

   - In one terminal:

```
bash

ros2 run ros2_publisher_subscriber
simple_publisher
```

   - In another terminal (after sourcing your workspace):

```
bash

ros2 run ros2_publisher_subscriber
simple_subscriber
```

8. If everything's correct, the subscriber will print messages like "I heard: Hello from ROS2, count: 0", "I heard: ...count: 1", etc.

Publisher-Subscriber Node Setup

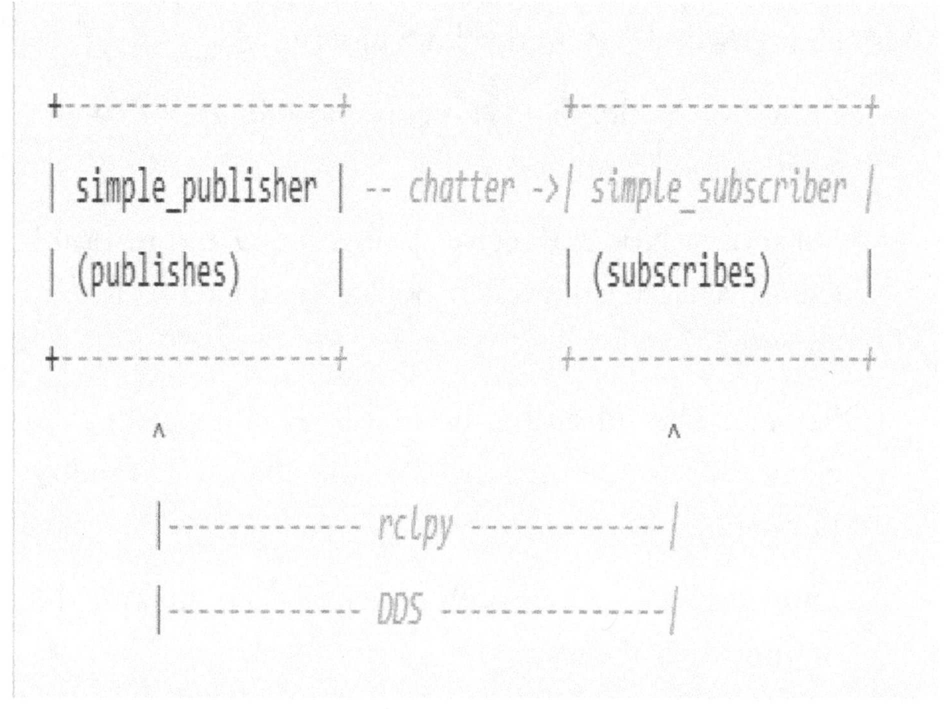

3.5. Hands-On Project: "Hello, Robot!" with ROS2 and Python

We've seen how to build a basic pub-sub system. Now, let's level it up slightly in a hands-on project called **"Hello, Robot!"** that demonstrates:

1. **Package organization**
2. **Launch file usage**
3. **A quick demonstration of services** (in addition to the pub-sub model)

3.5.1. Project Overview

Our "Hello, Robot!" system will include:

- **Publisher Node:** Sends greetings to the "robot" on a topic named /greeting.
- **Subscriber Node:** Receives that greeting and responds using a **service** call (the "robot" acknowledging the greeting).
- **Service:** The subscriber node will act as a service **client**, calling a service that logs the response "Hello, Human!"
- **Launch File:** To start both nodes at once, making the demonstration easier.

3.5.2. Step-by-Step Guide

1. **Create a New Package** (Or reuse the existing pub-sub package if you prefer. For clarity, we'll make a new one.)

```
bash


cd ~/ros2_ws/src
ros2 pkg create hello_robot --build-type
ament_python
```

2. **Project Structure**
   The generated folder hello_robot will contain:

```
arduino
```

```
hello_robot/
├── package.xml
├── setup.py
└── hello_robot
    ├── __init__.py
    ├── greeting_publisher.py
    └── robot_subscriber.py
```

3. **Write the Publisher Node (greeting_publisher.py)**

```
python

#!/usr/bin/env python3

import rclpy
from rclpy.node import Node
from std_msgs.msg import String

class GreetingPublisher(Node):
    def __init__(self):
        super().__init__('greeting_publisher')
        self.pub_ = self.create_publisher(String,
'/greeting', 10)
        self.timer = self.create_timer(2.0,
self.publish_greeting)
        self.get_logger().info("Greeting
Publisher Node has started.")

    def publish_greeting(self):
```

```
        msg = String()
        msg.data = "Hello, Robot!"
        self.pub_.publish(msg)
        self.get_logger().info(f"Publishing:
{msg.data}")

def main(args=None):
    rclpy.init(args=args)
    node = GreetingPublisher()
    rclpy.spin(node)
    node.destroy_node()
    rclpy.shutdown()

if __name__ == '__main__':
    main()
```

Key Points:

- Publishes **"Hello, Robot!"** every **2 seconds.**
- Logs the message to the console for debugging.

4. **Write the Subscriber/Service Client Node (robot_subscriber.py)**

```
python

#!/usr/bin/env python3

import rclpy
from rclpy.node import Node
from std_msgs.msg import String
```

```
from example_interfaces.srv import Trigger  #
We'll use a standard Trigger service


class RobotSubscriber(Node):
    def __init__(self):
        super().__init__('robot_subscriber')
        self.sub_ = self.create_subscription(
            String,
            '/greeting',
            self.greeting_callback,
            10
        )
        self.client_ =
self.create_client(Trigger, '/robot_response')
        self.get_logger().info("Robot Subscriber
Node has started.")

    def greeting_callback(self, msg):
        self.get_logger().info(f"Robot heard:
{msg.data}")
        if msg.data.lower().startswith("hello"):
            # Robot calls the service to respond
            self.call_robot_service()

    def call_robot_service(self):
        while not
self.client_.wait_for_service(timeout_sec=1.0):
```

```
            self.get_logger().info("Service
/robot_response not available, waiting...")

        request = Trigger.Request()
        self.client_.call_async(request)

def main(args=None):
    rclpy.init(args=args)
    node = RobotSubscriber()
    rclpy.spin(node)
    node.destroy_node()
    rclpy.shutdown()

if __name__ == '__main__':
    main()
```

Key Points:

- Subscribes to /greeting. Every time it receives a message starting with **"hello"**, it attempts to call a service named /robot_response.
- Uses example_interfaces/srv/Trigger as a generic service. This service type has no inputs except a request object and returns a simple boolean success and a message string.

5. **Write the Service Server (robot_responder.py)**

```
python

#!/usr/bin/env python3
```

```
import rclpy
from rclpy.node import Node
from example_interfaces.srv import Trigger

class RobotResponder(Node):
    def __init__(self):
        super().__init__('robot_responder')
        self.srv_ = self.create_service(Trigger,
'/robot_response', self.response_callback)
        self.get_logger().info("Robot Responder
Service has started.")

    def response_callback(self, request,
response):
        self.get_logger().info("Responding to
greeting...")
        response.success = True
        response.message = "Hello, Human! (From
Robot)"
        return response

def main(args=None):
    rclpy.init(args=args)
    node = RobotResponder()
    rclpy.spin(node)
    node.destroy_node()
    rclpy.shutdown()
```

```
if __name__ == '__main__':
    main()
```

Key Points:

- Advertises a service on /robot_response.
- When triggered, it returns "Hello, Human! (From Robot)" to the caller.
- Notice how Trigger.srv is **service-based**—the node waits for a request, processes it, and returns a response.

6. **Add Entry Points in setup.py**

```
python

from setuptools import setup

package_name = 'hello_robot'

setup(
    name=package_name,
    version='0.0.0',
    packages=[package_name],
    data_files=[

('share/ament_index/resource_index/packages',
            ['resource/' + package_name]),
```

```
        ('share/' + package_name,
['package.xml']),
    ],
    install_requires=['setuptools'],
    zip_safe=True,
    maintainer='YourName',
    maintainer_email='YourEmail@example.com',
    description='Hello, Robot! demo with pub-sub
and service',
    license='Apache License 2.0',
    tests_require=['pytest'],
    entry_points={
        'console_scripts': [
            'greeting_publisher =
hello_robot.greeting_publisher:main',
            'robot_subscriber =
hello_robot.robot_subscriber:main',
            'robot_responder =
hello_robot.robot_responder:main',
        ],
    },
)
```

7. **Create a Launch File** (inside hello_robot/hello_robot named hello_robot.launch.py):

```
python

from launch import LaunchDescription
from launch_ros.actions import Node
```

```
def generate_launch_description():
    return LaunchDescription([
        Node(
            package='hello_robot',
            executable='greeting_publisher',
            name='greeting_publisher'
        ),
        Node(
            package='hello_robot',
            executable='robot_subscriber',
            name='robot_subscriber'
        ),
        Node(
            package='hello_robot',
            executable='robot_responder',
            name='robot_responder'
        ),
    ])
```

Explanation:

- The launch file starts all three nodes:
    1. greeting_publisher (publishes "Hello, Robot!" periodically)
    2. robot_subscriber (subscribes to the greeting, calls the service if the greeting starts with "hello")

3. robot_responder (handles the service request and replies "Hello, Human!")

8. **Build and Run**

```
bash


cd ~/ros2_ws
colcon build
source install/setup.bash


ros2 launch hello_robot hello_robot.launch.py
```

Expected Console Output:

- greeting_publisher logs: "Publishing: Hello, Robot!" every 2 seconds.
- robot_subscriber logs: "Robot heard: Hello, Robot!" each time it receives a message.
- robot_responder logs: "Responding to greeting..." whenever it's called, and internally returns "Hello, Human!" to the subscriber.

"Hello, Robot!" System

```
+-------------+  Publish: "Hello, Robot!"
| Publisher   | ---------------------------------> /greeting
| (Greeting)  |
+-------------+

+-------------+  Subscribe /greeting  +-------------+
| Subscriber  | ----------------------> | Responder   |
| (Robot)     |                        | (Service)   |
|    +--- Service Client --- /robot_response --> Srv ---+
+-------------+
```

When the subscriber node hears "Hello, Robot!", it immediately calls the /robot_response service, which triggers a friendly response from the Responder node.

3.5.3. Variations and Further Exploration

- **Add a Timer** in robot_subscriber to send the service request on an interval, not just on receiving a message.
- **QoS Tweaks**: Experiment with reliability or durability settings in your publisher and subscriber to see how it affects message delivery.
- **Parameters**: Use ROS2 parameters to configure how often greetings are published, or to change the text at runtime.

Wrapping Up Chapter 3

We've covered a lot of ground here:

1. **Nodes:** The heart of ROS2, each handling a specific slice of robot functionality.
2. **Topics:** The backbone for sending and receiving **streams** of data, from sensor readings to motion commands.
3. **Services:** For **request-response** style tasks, where a node calls another node and awaits a direct reply.
4. **Actions:** Ideal for **long-running** tasks requiring **progress updates** or the ability to **cancel** mid-way.
5. **Message Passing:** The robust, type-safe system that ensures nodes get the data they need, courtesy of DDS behind the scenes.
6. **Packages and Launch Files:** The organizational framework that keeps your code tidy and orchestrates multi-node setups.
7. **Real-World Example:** A straightforward publisher-subscriber demonstration, plus our **"Hello, Robot!"** project integrating services for a more interactive demonstration.

Key Takeaways

- **ROS2's Pub-Sub Paradigm**: Decoupling publishers and subscribers leads to flexible, scalable robotics software.
- **Services and Actions**: Expand on simple data streams by enabling synchronous calls and handling long tasks with feedback.
- **Package Organization**: Group related nodes, message types, and launch files under a single package for easier distribution and maintenance.
- **Launch Files**: An indispensable tool for bootstrapping complex systems.
- **Hands-On Learning**: Building the "Hello, Robot!" example cements conceptual knowledge into practical skill.

Troubleshooting & FAQ

1. **Q**: "I ran ros2 run hello_robot greeting_publisher but got Command not found."
   A: Ensure you've rebuilt and sourced your workspace:

```
bash


colcon build
source install/setup.bash
```

Also verify that entry_points in setup.py is correct and matches your script filenames.

2. **Q**: "My subscriber doesn't receive messages. Why?"
   A: Double-check the **topic name** and **message type**. If either differs between publisher and subscriber, the communication won't occur. Also ensure both nodes are running in the same ROS2 domain (by default, domain zero).

3. **Q**: "How do I see a list of all topics in the system?"
   A: Use:

```bash
ros2 topic list
```

Then, for more detail:

```bash
ros2 topic info /greeting
```

4. **Q**: "Why choose actions over services for a certain task?"
   A: If the task takes significant time (e.g., navigation across a warehouse) and you want progress updates or the option to cancel mid-task, choose actions. Services are best for quick requests where immediate completion is expected.

5. **Q**: "Where do custom messages fit in?"
   A: If you find yourself needing specialized data (e.g., a struct with multiple sensor readings), create a new .msg file in your package and reference it in your code.

After building, ROS2 auto-generates code for that custom message type.

Next Steps

- In **Chapter 4: Python Essentials for Robotics**, we'll deepen our Python knowledge—covering best practices, libraries, and debugging techniques specifically tailored to robotics.
- Keep iterating on your "Hello, Robot!" project, perhaps adding sensors or real hardware. The upcoming chapters will introduce you to **robot architecture** and **hardware fundamentals**, so you can eventually move from simulation to a physical robot.

Remember: Mastery of these basics—**nodes, topics, services, actions, launch files, and packages**—is the key to building any advanced robotic system in ROS2. Whether it's a simple home project or a complex industrial robot, these same principles apply.

Chapter 4: Python Essentials for Robotics

If you've made it this far, you already know that **Python** has become a cornerstone of modern robotics—thanks to its simplicity, readability, and extensive ecosystem of libraries. But how exactly do you apply Python for sensor data processing, real-time troubleshooting, and AI-driven automation in your robotic systems? That's exactly what we'll explore in this chapter.

We'll follow a **step-by-step approach** to cover the basics, from Python syntax and object-oriented design to advanced libraries like **NumPy**, **OpenCV**, and **SciPy**. We'll also delve into **error handling** and **debugging**, rounding things off with a **hands-on project** where you'll build a simple yet powerful sensor data processor. Throughout, we'll keep it jargon-free, interspersed with analogies and rhetorical questions to keep things engaging.

By the end of this chapter, you'll be fully equipped to leverage Python for tasks ranging from real-time data collection to robust, modular code design. Whether you're an aspiring hobbyist or a professional developer, these Pythonic insights will serve as a foundation for all your robotics endeavors.

4.1. Quick Refresher on Python Syntax and Concepts

This section provides a brief recap of Python fundamentals that are especially relevant in robotics. If you're already comfortable with Python, skim through for any robotics-specific tips you might've missed. If you're new, consider it a concise crash course.

4.1.1 Variables and Data Types

In robotics, you'll frequently store and manipulate **sensor readings**, **configuration parameters**, and more. Python's flexible variables and dynamic typing make it easy to handle diverse data.

1. **Numbers**

```
python


temperature = 23.5      # float
motor_speed = 10        # int
```

- Floats are invaluable for sensor data, which often comes in decimal form.
- Integers may handle discrete steps or iteration counters.

2. **Strings**

```
python
```

```
robot_name = "MarsRover"
```

- Commonly used for debugging messages, logging, or labeling sensor data.

3. **Booleans**

```python
is_operational = True
```

- Perfect for checks like "Is the motor overheated?" or "Is the robot connected to Wi-Fi?"

4. **Lists and Tuples**

```python
sensor_readings = [23.5, 24.1, 24.7]      # list
position = (12.0, 5.6, 7.3)               # tuple
(x, y, z)
```

- **Lists** are mutable (you can add, remove, or modify elements).
- **Tuples** are immutable—useful for fixed-size data like coordinates or dimension specifications.

5. **Dictionaries**

```python
sensor_data = {
    "temperature": 23.5,
    "humidity": 45.2,
```

```
    "pressure": 1012
}
```

- Maps keys to values—ideal for grouping sensor readings by name.

4.1.2 Control Flow and Loops

Robotics often demands real-time checks, data polling, and repeated calculations. Python's control structures help you handle these gracefully.

1. **if-elif-else**

```python
if temperature > 40:
    print("Warning: Overheated!")
elif temperature < 0:
    print("Warning: Freezing!")
else:
    print("Temperature is normal.")
```

- Great for conditional logic like safety checks.

2. **for Loops**

```python
for reading in sensor_readings:
    print(f"Reading: {reading}")
```

- Typically used to iterate over lists or dictionaries.

3. **while Loops**

python

```python
while is_operational:
    # Read sensor, publish data, etc.
    ...
```

   - Handy for continuous loops where you're polling sensors until a condition changes.

4.1.3 Functions

In robotics, modularity is key—grouping related logic into **functions** clarifies code and encourages reuse.

python

```python
def compute_avg(values):
  if not values:
        return 0.0
    return sum(values) / len(values)
```

- Functions can handle specific tasks, like **calculating an average sensor reading**, or controlling a **drive motor**.
- Combine them with libraries to make your code more readable and maintainable.

4.1.4 Modules and Packages

As soon as your code grows beyond a few hundred lines, you'll benefit from **modules** (single Python files) and **packages** (folders with multiple modules).

- **Example:** You might place all motor-related code in motor_control.py and all sensor-related code in sensors.py.
- This separation keeps your code manageable and fosters collaborative development.

Diagram 4.1: Basic Python Project Structure for Robotics

```
my_robot/
 ├─ sensor_utils.py       (module for sensor handling)
 ├─ motor_controller.py   (module for motor commands)
 ├─ main.py               (entry point)
 ├─ config/
 │    └─ robot_params.json
 └─ tests/
      └─ test_sensors.py
```

This diagram illustrates a simplified layout where sensor_utils.py and motor_controller.py each tackle a core aspect of the robot, while main.py orchestrates everything.

4.2. Object-Oriented Programming (OOP) for Robotic Components

Object-Oriented Programming (OOP) may sound abstract, but in robotics, it's incredibly practical. **A robot is composed of multiple subsystems**—sensors, actuators, communication modules—and OOP helps you model each subsystem as a class.

4.2.1 Classes and Objects in Robotics

1. **Classes**: A blueprint describing what attributes (data) and behaviors (functions) a particular subsystem has.
2. **Objects**: Actual **instances** of those classes. For example, you can have multiple sensor objects (e.g., front_lidar, rear_lidar) each built from a LidarSensor class.

4.2.2 Example: A LidarSensor Class

Let's create a hypothetical LidarSensor class to see how OOP might look in a robotics context.

python

```
class LidarSensor:
```

```
    def __init__(self, model, max_range, port):
        self.model = model
        self.max_range = max_range
        self.port = port
        self.data = []

    def connect(self):
        # Code to initialize a serial or USB
connection
        print(f"Connecting {self.model} on port
{self.port}")

    def read_data(self):
        # Code to read raw data from the sensor
        # For simplicity, we'll simulate random
data
        import random
        self.data = [random.uniform(0,
self.max_range) for _ in range(360)]
        return self.data

    def process_data(self):
        # Example: Find minimum distance in the
360-degree scan
        if not self.data:
            return None
        return min(self.data)
```

Key Points:

- **Constructor (__init__)**: Sets up sensor properties like model name, range, and communication port.
- **connect()**: Establishes a communication link with the actual hardware or simulator.
- **read_data()**: Retrieves sensor measurements, storing them in self.data.
- **process_data()**: Applies an algorithm, like finding the closest obstacle.

By **encapsulating** all LiDAR logic in one class, you keep your code organized, testable, and easily reusable for different LiDAR models.

4.2.3 Inheritance and Polymorphism

If your robot has multiple sensor types (LiDAR, sonar, camera), you might want them to share certain methods (like connect()), but each could have unique specifics. **Inheritance** helps:

```
python


class Sensor:
    def __init__(self, model):
        self.model = model


    def connect(self):
        raise NotImplementedError("Subclass must
implement this method.")
```

```
class LidarSensor(Sensor):
    def __init__(self, model, max_range, port):
        super().__init__(model)
        self.max_range = max_range
        self.port = port
        self.data = []

    def connect(self):
        print(f"Connecting LiDAR sensor
{self.model} on port {self.port}")
```

Polymorphism allows you to treat objects of different sensor types with the same interface—handy for code that processes sensors without caring about their internals.

4.2.4 Designing Robotic Systems with Classes

Object-orientation encourages you to think about each subsystem as an entity with **data** (attributes) and **capabilities** (methods). This becomes invaluable as your robot's complexity grows. For example, you can easily coordinate multiple OOP-based components like:

- A MotorController that handles wheel velocities.
- A CameraSensor that processes frames.
- A NavigationModule that fuses data from sensors to plan paths.

OOP Design for a Simple Robot

```
my_robot/
 ├─ sensor_utils.py       (module for sensor handling)
 ├─ motor_controller.py   (module for motor commands)
 ├─ main.py               (entry point)
 ├─ config/
 │   └─ robot_params.json
 └─ tests/
     └─ test_sensors.py
```

This hierarchical approach keeps each component self-contained, simplifying both collaboration and debugging.

4.3. Python Libraries for Robotics (NumPy, OpenCV, SciPy)

Beyond the language fundamentals, robotics demands specialized functions: matrix operations, image processing, signal analysis, and more. Python's **ecosystem** offers robust libraries that accelerate these tasks.

4.3.1 NumPy for Numerical Computations

Why NumPy? Robotics often involves vector and matrix math—2D transformations, 3D transformations, state estimation, you name it. **NumPy** is the go-to library for fast, vectorized computations.

```
python

import numpy as np

# Example: 2D transformation
points = np.array([[1.0, 2.0], [3.0, 4.0]])  #
shape (2,2)
transform_matrix = np.array([[0, -1],
                             [1,  0]])
rotated_points = points @ transform_matrix
print(rotated_points)
```

Key Features:

1. **Arrays** are more efficient than standard Python lists for large data sets.
2. **Broadcasting** allows simple syntax for complex operations.
3. **Linear Algebra** (matrix multiplications, inversions) is built-in, saving you from re-inventing the wheel.

4.3.2 OpenCV for Computer Vision

- **Why OpenCV?** Computer Vision is huge in robotics—detecting obstacles, recognizing objects, or calibrating cameras. **OpenCV** (Open Source Computer Vision) is a comprehensive library with everything from basic image processing to advanced machine learning modules.

```python
import cv2

def detect_edges(frame):
    gray = cv2.cvtColor(frame,
cv2.COLOR_BGR2GRAY)
    edges = cv2.Canny(gray, 50, 150)
    return edges

# Example usage in a loop:
cap = cv2.VideoCapture(0)  # open a camera
while True:
    ret, frame = cap.read()
    if not ret:
        break

    edges = detect_edges(frame)
    cv2.imshow("Edges", edges)
```

```
    if cv2.waitKey(1) & 0xFF == ord('q'):
        break

cap.release()
cv2.destroyAllWindows()
```

Features:

1. **Image/Video I/O**: Access cameras, read or write video files, and display images in real-time.
2. **Image Processing**: Filters, edge detection, color space conversions, etc.
3. **Object Recognition**: Haar cascades, deep learning frameworks, and more.

4.3.3 SciPy for Scientific Computing

- **Why SciPy? SciPy** extends NumPy with additional modules for optimization, interpolation, signal processing, and more advanced math—perfect for tasks like:
    1. **Sensor Fusion**: Filtering out noise or merging multiple data streams.
    2. **Control Systems**: If you're implementing PID controllers or advanced control strategies.
    3. **Optimization**: Fine-tuning parameters for your robot's motion planning or joint angles.

```
python
```

```
from scipy import optimize

# Example: Minimizing a simple function
def objective(x):
    return x**2 + 3*x + 4

result = optimize.minimize(objective, x0=0)
print(result.x)   # The x value that minimizes
the function
```

Combine **SciPy** with **NumPy** and you have a robust toolkit for the math-heavy parts of robotics, from path planning to sensor data filtering.

4.3.4 Other Notable Libraries

1. **Matplotlib** or **Plotly**: Plot sensor data and debug numerical issues.
2. **Pandas**: Manage large data sets or time-series logs from extended robot runs.
3. **TensorFlow / PyTorch**: Dive into deep learning for advanced perception or decision-making.

4.4. Error Handling, Debugging, and Best Practices

Robotics code can fail in unpredictable ways: sensors might misbehave, hardware connections might drop, or unexpected data might blow up your algorithms. This section focuses on writing robust, maintainable Python code that **recovers gracefully**.

4.4.1 Exceptions and Try-Except Blocks

When dealing with real hardware or complex computations, **exceptions** are inevitable. Embrace them by handling errors thoughtfully:

```python
def read_sensor_data(sensor):
    try:
        data = sensor.read_data()  # might raise an IOError if sensor fails
    if data is None:
            raise ValueError("No data received from sensor.")
        return data
    except IOError as e:
        print(f"IOError: {str(e)}")
        return []
    except ValueError as ve:
        print(f"ValueError: {str(ve)}")
        return []
```

Tips:

- Use **specific** exceptions (e.g., IOError, ValueError) so you don't mask unexpected errors.

- Provide **meaningful error messages** to help with quick diagnosis.
- In mission-critical systems, you might need to fallback to a safe state or switch to redundant sensors if one fails.

4.4.2 Debugging Tools

1. **Logging**: Python's built-in logging module is more versatile than print statements.

```
python

import logging
logging.basicConfig(level=logging.DEBUG)
logging.debug("Debug info: sensor data reading
started.")
logging.info("Robot operational.")
logging.warning("Low battery!")
logging.error("Motor controller offline!")
```

2. **Breakpoints:** Tools like **pdb** or IDE debuggers let you pause execution and inspect variables.
3. **Visual Aids:** Plot sensor data using **Matplotlib** to spot anomalies quickly.

4.4.3 Best Practices for Clean, Maintainable Code

1. **PEP 8 Style:** Follow conventions for naming, spacing, and line length. This ensures everyone reads your code more easily.
2. **Modular Functions:** Each function should do one thing well—makes debugging simpler.
3. **Documentation:** Docstrings at the top of functions or classes to clarify usage.
4. **Unit Tests:** Test your modules individually to catch bugs early. Tools like **pytest** or **unittest** can automate this.
5. **Version Control:** Use **Git** (discussed in previous chapters) to track changes, revert to stable commits, and collaborate effectively.

4.4.4 Handling Real-Time Constraints

While Python is not typically your first choice for hard real-time tasks (C++ or embedded code often excels here), you can still handle many robotics tasks. Keep in mind:

- **Threading** or **multiprocessing** can help if you have multiple tasks that can run concurrently.
- For more stringent real-time performance, you might rely on a real-time OS or couple Python with lower-level code in C++.

4.5. Hands-On Project: A Simple Sensor Data Processor

Let's put these concepts into practice by **building a small Python tool** that reads from a (simulated) sensor, processes the data, and visualizes it in real-time. This project is minimal yet illustrative, combining everything we've discussed—**functions, OOP, libraries, error handling**, and **best practices**.

4.5.1 Project Overview

Imagine you have a temperature sensor that outputs readings in real-time. You want to:

1. **Read** the temperature at a fixed interval.
2. **Filter** out noise (using a simple moving average).
3. **Plot** the temperature history so you can see trends at a glance.

We'll simulate sensor data with random values for demonstration, but you can replace that part with actual sensor reads.

Diagram 4.3: Flow of Our Sensor Data Processor

```
[ Simulated Sensor ] --> [ Data Reader ] --> [ Noise Filtering ] --> [ Plotter / Monitor ]
```

4.5.2 Setting Up the Project Structure

1. **Create a Folder:**

```bash
mkdir sensor_processor
cd sensor_processor
```

2. **Inside** this folder, create these files:

```scss
sensor_processor/
├── sensor.py              (Simulated sensor class)
├── processor.py           (Filtering and plotting logic)
├── main.py                (Entry point)
├── requirements.txt       (Dependencies)
└── README.md              (Documentation)
```

4.5.3 sensor.py

```python
import random
import time

class SimulatedTemperatureSensor:
    def __init__(self, base_temp=25.0):
```

```
        self.base_temp = base_temp

    def read_temperature(self):
        # Simulate a slight random fluctuation
around base_temp
        noise = random.uniform(-2.0, 2.0)
        return self.base_temp + noise

    def get_timestamp(self):
        return time.time()
```

Explanation:

- base_temp simulates a normal operating temperature (25.0°C).
- read_temperature() returns a float with random noise to mimic real sensor data.
- get_timestamp() captures the current system time, which is useful for logging or plotting.

4.5.4 processor.py

This file will handle:

1. **Moving Average Filter**
2. **Matplotlib** real-time plotting

```
python

import collections
import matplotlib.pyplot as plt
```

```
import numpy as np

class DataProcessor:
    def __init__(self, window_size=5):
        # We'll keep a fixed-length deque for the
moving average
        self.window_size = window_size
        self.recent_readings =
collections.deque(maxlen=window_size)
        self.timestamps = []
        self.raw_values = []
        self.filtered_values = []

        # Setup Matplotlib
        plt.ion()  # interactive mode on
        self.fig, self.ax = plt.subplots()
        self.line_raw, = self.ax.plot([], [], 'r-
', label='Raw')
        self.line_filtered, = self.ax.plot([],
[], 'b-', label='Filtered')
        self.ax.legend()
        self.ax.set_xlabel('Time (s)')
        self.ax.set_ylabel('Temperature (°C)')
        self.ax.set_title('Real-Time Temperature
Data')

    def moving_average(self, new_value):
        self.recent_readings.append(new_value)
```

```
        return np.mean(self.recent_readings)

    def update_plot(self, time_val, raw_val,
filtered_val):
        # Append new data to lists
        self.timestamps.append(time_val)
        self.raw_values.append(raw_val)
        self.filtered_values.append(filtered_val)

        # Update the line data
        self.line_raw.set_xdata(self.timestamps)
        self.line_raw.set_ydata(self.raw_values)

self.line_filtered.set_xdata(self.timestamps)

self.line_filtered.set_ydata(self.filtered_values
)

        # Adjust plot limits
        self.ax.relim()
        self.ax.autoscale_view()

        # Redraw
        plt.draw()
        plt.pause(0.01)
```

Key Points:

- We use a **deque** for the **moving average** filter. When a new temperature value arrives, we append it, drop the oldest if the deque is full, and compute the average.
- **Real-Time Plotting** is achieved by **Matplotlib** in interactive mode. We continuously update line data and call plt.draw() and plt.pause() to refresh the plot.

4.5.5 main.py

Here, we'll tie everything together.

python

```
import time
from sensor import SimulatedTemperatureSensor
from processor import DataProcessor

def main():
    sensor =
SimulatedTemperatureSensor(base_temp=25.0)
    processor = DataProcessor(window_size=5)

    print("Starting sensor data processing. Press
Ctrl+C to stop.")
    try:
        while True:
            # Read simulated sensor data
            temperature =
sensor.read_temperature()
```

```
            timestamp = sensor.get_timestamp()

            # Filter the data
            filtered_temp =
processor.moving_average(temperature)

            # Update the real-time plot
            processor.update_plot(timestamp,
temperature, filtered_temp)

            time.sleep(1.0)  # read at 1-second
intervals
    except KeyboardInterrupt:
        print("Shutting down sensor data
processing.")

if __name__ == "__main__":
    main()
```

Workflow:

1. **Initialize** a SimulatedTemperatureSensor and a DataProcessor.
2. **Continuous Loop**:
    - Grab the current temperature and timestamp.
    - Pass the temperature to the moving average filter.
    - Update the real-time Matplotlib plot.

3. **Graceful Exit** on Ctrl+C.

4.5.6 Installing Dependencies

In requirements.txt, you can list:

```
matplotlib
numpy
```

(If you're using **Python 3.8+** or a virtual environment, install with pip install -r requirements.txt.)

4.5.7 Testing the Project

1. **Run:**

```bash
python main.py
```

2. A **Matplotlib window** should appear, updating every second with both raw (red line) and filtered (blue line) temperature readings.

3. **Terminate** with Ctrl+C or by closing the plot window.

4.5.8 Possible Enhancements

- **Sensor Abstraction:** Switch from the simulated sensor to a real sensor by modifying the read_temperature() method.
- **Multi-Sensor:** Expand to handle multiple sensors by introducing more classes or threading.

- **Parameterization:** Create a config file for specifying base_temp, window_size, or sampling intervals.
- **Long-Term Logging:** Save data to disk (CSV or database) for post-run analysis.

Conclusion of Chapter 4

We've traversed the crucial Python essentials that form the **backbone** of many robotics projects. Starting with a syntax refresher, we explored how **object-oriented principles** can structure complex robotic systems into modular, reusable components. We then showcased how libraries like **NumPy**, **OpenCV**, and **SciPy** empower developers to efficiently handle data processing, computer vision, and advanced math. Finally, we dug into **best practices** for error handling and debugging, culminating in a **hands-on sensor data processing project.**

Key Takeaways

1. **Python Fundamentals:** Variables, loops, and functions might seem simple, but mastering them is critical for writing clean, efficient robotics code.
2. **OOP:** Classes help encapsulate each subsystem (sensor, controller, etc.), promoting clarity and reusability.

3. **Libraries: NumPy**, **OpenCV**, and **SciPy** unlock advanced capabilities, from matrix math to image processing to signal analysis.
4. **Error Handling:** Use exceptions and logging for robust, maintainable code that can handle the unpredictability of real-world hardware.
5. **Hands-On Project:** Even a simple program can illustrate how to read, filter, and visualize sensor data in real time.

Frequently Asked Questions

1. **Q**: Can Python handle time-critical tasks in robotics?
   A: Python can address many near real-time tasks, especially on modern hardware. For true hard real-time guarantees, you'll typically pair Python with a lower-level language like C++, or use a real-time operating system.
2. **Q**: Are there simpler alternatives to Matplotlib for real-time plotting?
   A: Yes, **Plotly**, **PyQtGraph**, or specialized GUIs (like **Tkinter**) might provide more interactive real-time visualizations. But Matplotlib is a good starting point because it's widely documented.
3. **Q**: I'm concerned about CPU usage when using Python threads. Any tips?
   A: Python has the **Global Interpreter Lock (GIL)** that can limit true parallelism for CPU-bound tasks. For

CPU-heavy work, use **multiprocessing** (which spawns separate processes) or offload certain parts to C/C++ libraries.

4. **Q**: How do I integrate these Python scripts with ROS2?
   A: You can create a **ROS2 package** (as discussed in earlier chapters), put your Python scripts in src/ or a subfolder, and define **entry_points** in setup.py. Then you can run them with ros2 run package_name script_name.
5. **Q**: Where can I learn more about advanced filtering methods?
   A: Check out **SciPy**'s signal processing modules, **filterpy**, or **OpenCV** for more sophisticated noise reduction and sensor fusion algorithms.

What's Next?

With this solid grounding in Python essentials, you're prepared to tackle the next challenges of robotics:

- **Chapter 5: Robot Architecture and Hardware Fundamentals** will bring together software and physical components—sensors, actuators, microcontrollers—so you can start building tangible robotics projects.
- Continue enhancing your Python code with advanced libraries (e.g., TensorFlow for machine learning) and keep refining your debugging and testing strategies.

- If you haven't already, **experiment** with hooking your Python scripts into **ROS2** to harness the full capabilities of a distributed, modular robotics framework.

As always, keep iterating on your code, exploring new libraries, and embracing best practices. **In robotics, everything is iterative:** every sensor reading or system upgrade can lead to new insights and improvements. With Python as your trusted ally, you'll be ready to tackle an ever-expanding range of challenges—whether that's building a simple mobile rover or orchestrating a fleet of autonomous drones!

Chapter 5: Robot Architecture and Hardware Fundamentals

Robots aren't just about code and clever algorithms. At their core, they rely on **physical components**—from microcontrollers to sensors—to perceive and act on their environment. Understanding these hardware building blocks is crucial for anyone serious about robotics. Why do certain projects use Arduino boards while others opt for a Raspberry Pi? How do you wire an ultrasonic sensor to get distance measurements in ROS2? And what's the difference between UART, SPI, I2C, and CAN?

In this chapter, we'll **bridge the gap** between the software side of robotics (which you've been exploring in previous chapters) and the **physical hardware** that brings your robot to life. We'll tackle:

1. **Common Robotics Hardware**: Microcontrollers, Single-Board Computers (SBCs), and the array of sensors that feed data into your robot's "brain."
2. **Interfacing Sensors and Actuators with ROS2**: Practical ways to connect your hardware so that ROS2 nodes can read sensor data and control motors or servos.

3. **Communication Protocols**: A breakdown of **UART**, **SPI**, **I2C**, and **CAN**—the highways and byways of embedded systems.
4. **Hands-On Project**: Wiring and testing an **ultrasonic sensor** to measure distance, then integrating it with ROS2 so you can see real-time distance readings.
5. **Real-World Applications**: A look at how these hardware fundamentals power robots in **manufacturing**, **healthcare**, **logistics**, and other cutting-edge industries.

As always, we'll stick to a **conversational, jargon-free** style, using **step-by-step** explanations, **visual aids**, and relatable analogies. By the end of this chapter, you'll have a clear sense of how the hardware side of robotics fits together—and how to build or integrate those components into a functioning ROS2 system.

5.1. Common Robotics Hardware: Microcontrollers, SBCs, and Sensors

When you peel back the layers of any modern robot, you'll find **core electronic components** that handle processing, sensing, and actuation. Let's examine the usual suspects.

5.1.1 Microcontrollers (MCUs)

A **microcontroller** is essentially a small computer on a single integrated circuit, designed to handle specific control tasks. Examples include the **Arduino Uno**, **Teensy**, or **ESP32** boards. You typically program these MCUs in C/C++ (though MicroPython and other languages are on the rise), and they excel at **real-time** or near-real-time tasks with direct access to **GPIO pins**.

Why use a microcontroller?

1. **Deterministic Timing:** Many microcontrollers can operate with consistent timing loops, ideal for controlling motors, servos, or reading sensors that require precise timing.
2. **Low Power:** Great for battery-powered or energy-conscious applications.
3. **Simplicity:** Straightforward interfacing with digital and analog inputs.

Typical Use Cases:

- Controlling a set of DC motors or servos.
- Reading simple analog sensors (like potentiometers, thermistors) with built-in analog-to-digital converters (ADCs).
- Handling repetitive tasks such as blinking LEDs, measuring pulses, or generating PWM (Pulse Width Modulation) signals.

5.1.2 Single-Board Computers (SBCs)

Where a microcontroller is a "bare-bones" system, an **SBC** is a **full computer** in a compact form factor. Think **Raspberry Pi**, **NVIDIA Jetson Nano**, or **BeagleBone**. These typically run a **Linux** operating system and can handle more computationally heavy tasks, like **computer vision** or **machine learning**.

Advantages:

1. **OS Support:** With Linux, you have easy access to Python, ROS2, and advanced libraries (like OpenCV).
2. **Multi-Tasking:** Run multiple processes (e.g., a camera driver, a sensor fusion algorithm, and a ROS2 node) simultaneously.
3. **Connectivity:** Built-in Ethernet, Wi-Fi, and Bluetooth make it simple to network your robot.

Typical Use Cases:

- Running ROS2 with multiple nodes for perception, navigation, and behavior coordination.
- Hosting heavier computational tasks like real-time object detection or SLAM (Simultaneous Localization and Mapping).

- Acting as the main "brain" of the robot, often delegating simpler tasks to microcontrollers.

5.1.3 Sensors

Robots need **eyes, ears, and a sense of touch**—and that's where sensors come in. The sensor landscape is huge, but here are some common categories:

1. **Distance Sensors**
    - **Ultrasonic** (like the HC-SR04)
    - **Infrared** (short-range detection)
    - **LiDAR** (Laser-based scanning)
    - These measure proximity or distance to obstacles.
2. **Vision Sensors**
    - **Cameras** (2D or depth cameras)
    - **Thermal cameras** (for heat signatures)
    - Used in tasks ranging from object detection to visual odometry.
3. **IMUs (Inertial Measurement Units)**
    - Combine **accelerometers**, **gyroscopes**, and sometimes **magnetometers**.
    - Provide orientation, angular velocity, and acceleration data—crucial for stabilizing drones or tracking robot orientation.

4. **Encoders**
    - Typically attached to motors or wheels to measure **rotational movement** or **linear displacement.**
    - Vital for odometry calculations and controlling speed or position.
5. **Environmental Sensors**
    - Temperature, humidity, gas sensors, etc.
    - Used in specialized robots—like greenhouse robots or hazardous material handlers.

5.1.4 Actuators

Sensors bring in data; **actuators** do the work—motors, servos, stepper motors, and hydraulic systems. In many modern robots, you'll see:

1. **DC Motors** with or without gearboxes.
2. **Servo Motors** for controlled rotation within a limited angle (common in robotic arms).
3. **Stepper Motors** for precise control of position (e.g., 3D printers).
4. **Brushless Motors** (BLDC) for drones and high-performance tasks.

Selecting the right actuator depends on **torque requirements**, **speed**, **precision**, and **power availability**.

Basic Hardware Architecture

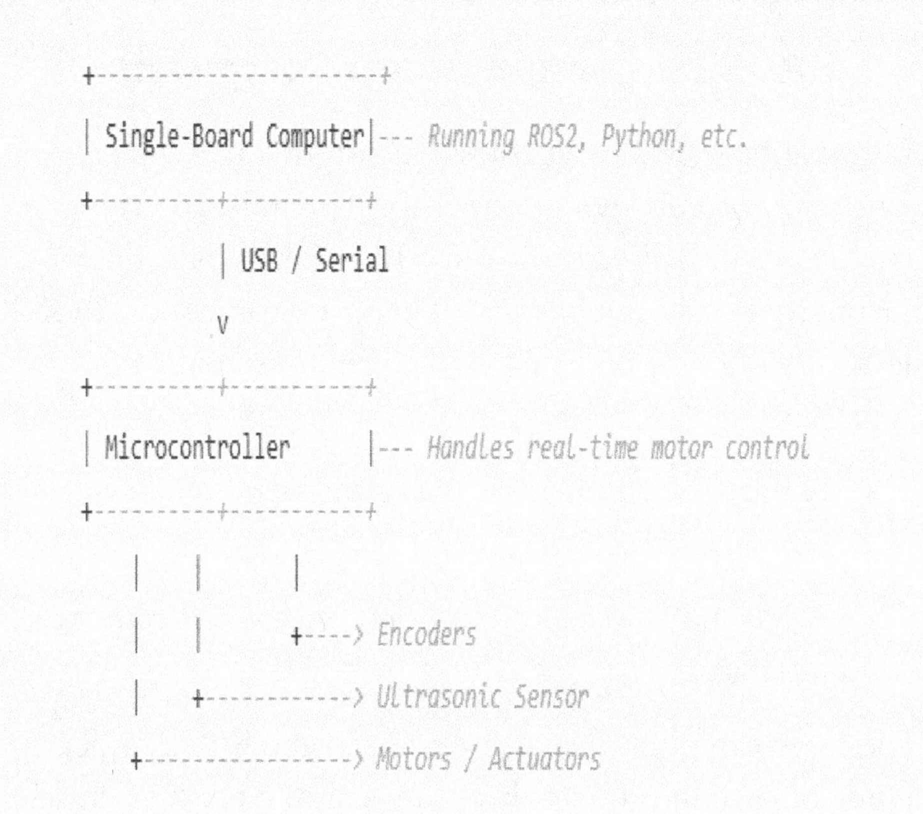

In this simplified diagram, the SBC handles high-level logic (e.g., SLAM, AI) while the microcontroller manages real-time sensor reads and motor drivers.

5.2. Interfacing Sensors and Actuators with ROS2

Now that you have an overview of hardware options, **how does ROS2 talk** to them? ROS2 itself runs in the higher-level OS (like Linux on a Raspberry Pi), while microcontrollers or other boards interface with hardware pins. Let's see how to bridge these worlds.

5.2.1 ROS2 on Single-Board Computers

Easiest approach: If your robot has no strict real-time constraints or only moderate sensor demands, you can connect sensors **directly** to your SBC's GPIO pins (like a Raspberry Pi's 40-pin header). Then, you can write a **ROS2 node** in Python or C++ that reads from those pins. For example:

- A Raspberry Pi reading from **I2C** sensors (like a temperature sensor).
- A Jetson Nano capturing video from a CSI camera interface.

The node can publish sensor readings on a ROS2 topic, letting other nodes (possibly on the same or another device) subscribe to that data.

5.2.2 ROS2 with Microcontrollers

If your design calls for a microcontroller to handle time-critical tasks or gather sensor data, you can use a **ROS2 "bridge"** or **middleware** that runs on both ends:

1. **Micro ROS**: A project that brings the ROS2 client libraries onto microcontrollers like the STM32 or ESP32. This way, the MCU becomes a **first-class ROS2 node**.

2. **Serial Bridges:** If your microcontroller doesn't directly support micro-ROS, you could write custom firmware that sends sensor data over serial (UART, USB) to the SBC. A node on the SBC reads this data, packages it into ROS2 messages, and publishes it.

5.2.3 Interfacing Actuators

If your SBC can handle the current requirements (often via a motor driver board or HAT), you can send **PWM signals** directly from the SBC's GPIO. Alternatively, your microcontroller can do the PWM generation, receiving commands from the SBC via a topic or service call.

Example:

- A node on the SBC receives velocity commands (like geometry_msgs/msg/Twist).
- It sends these commands to the microcontroller over serial.
- The microcontroller sets the appropriate PWM signals for the motors.

Integration Tip: Keep your signals safe. Motors can draw large currents and cause voltage spikes, so you typically separate high-power lines from sensitive signal lines. Use motor driver boards or dedicated ESCs (Electronic Speed Controllers) that protect the logic side from the motor side.

5.3. Communication Protocols (UART, SPI, I2C, CAN)

Behind every sensor reading or motor command is a **communication protocol** that orchestrates data flow. These protocols operate at the hardware and low-level software layers, ensuring bits travel from one chip to another accurately. Let's look at the key players.

5.3.1 UART (Universal Asynchronous Receiver/Transmitter)

- **Nature**: Serial protocol with **TX** (transmit) and **RX** (receive) lines.
- **Speed**: Common baud rates include 9600, 115200, 500000, etc.
- **Topology**: Point-to-point communication between two devices (e.g., microcontroller to a sensor or to an SBC over USB-to-serial).

Pros:

- Very simple to implement.
- Widely used (almost every microcontroller has UART pins).

Cons:

- Not great for multi-device on the same line (only 1-to-1).

- Relatively low speed compared to SPI or USB 2.0.

5.3.2 SPI (Serial Peripheral Interface)

- **Nature:** Synchronous serial protocol with **MOSI** (Master Out Slave In), **MISO** (Master In Slave Out), **SCLK** (clock), and **CS** (chip select) lines.
- **Speed:** Can be quite fast (several MHz).
- **Topology:** One master (usually the SBC or microcontroller), multiple slaves (sensors, displays, etc.).

Pros:

- High-speed data transfer.
- Good for devices that need fast updates (like certain displays or sensors).

Cons:

- Requires multiple lines (MISO, MOSI, SCLK, plus a CS line per device).
- Not hot-swappable, and cable lengths are typically short.

5.3.3 I2C (Inter-Integrated Circuit)

- **Nature:** Two-wire interface–**SDA** (data) and **SCL** (clock).

- **Speed**: Standard up to 100kHz (some can do 400kHz or 1MHz "Fast Mode"), suitable for moderate-speed sensors.
- **Topology**: Multi-slave bus, each device has an **address**.

Pros:

- Only two wires needed (plus power and ground).
- Easy to add multiple devices on the same bus.

Cons:

- Limited cable lengths, typically a few meters max.
- Speed is slower than SPI, so not ideal for large data transfers.

5.3.4 CAN (Controller Area Network)

- **Nature**: Multi-master bus, heavily used in **automotive** and **industrial** robotics.
- **Speed**: Often up to 1 Mbps (Classical CAN); can go higher with CAN FD.
- **Topology**: Nodes connected on a shared differential pair, each with a unique ID in messages.

Pros:

- Very robust against noise (differential signaling).
- Great for complex systems with many devices.
- Error detection and collision resolution built-in.

Cons:

- More complex to set up than UART or I2C.
- Requires transceivers and sometimes specialized library support.

Common Communication Protocols

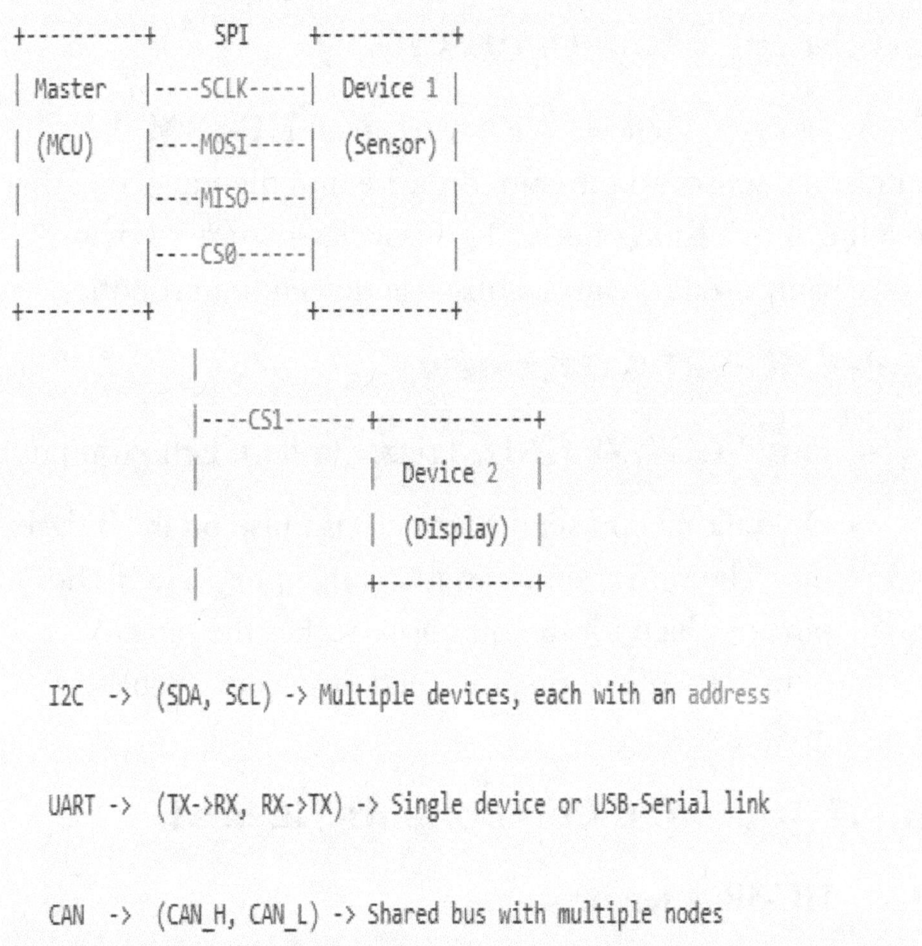

This schematic highlights how different protocols handle data transfer. SPI typically needs more wires but offers higher speeds and dedicated lines. I2C, with just two wires, is simpler but slower.

5.4. Hands-On Project: Wiring and Testing an Ultrasonic Sensor for Distance Measurement

Now, let's get practical. We'll wire up an **HC-SR04 ultrasonic sensor** to measure distance and then integrate that reading into a **ROS2 node**. This is a classic starter sensor, commonly used for simple obstacle detection in robotics.

5.4.1 HC-SR04 Overview

- **Pins**: VCC (5V), GND, **Trigger** (input), **Echo** (output).
- **Operation**: You send a brief 10µs pulse on the Trigger pin. The sensor emits an ultrasonic ping. The Echo pin goes high for the duration it takes the ping to return. By measuring this high-time, you calculate distance.

5.4.2 Tools and Components Needed

1. **HC-SR04 sensor**
2. **Microcontroller** (e.g., Arduino Uno) or a single-board computer with a real-time capable pin for measuring pulses.
3. **Breadboard** and **jumper wires**

4. Optional: A **logic level shifter** if your microcontroller uses 3.3V logic but the sensor is 5V (some boards require this for safe interfacing).

5.4.3 Wiring Diagram

HC-SR04 to Arduino Wiring

```
Arduino UNO              HC-SR04

5V  ---------------- VCC

GND ---------------- GND

Digital Pin 9 ----- TRIG

Digital Pin 8 ----- ECHO
```

If you're using a Raspberry Pi (3.3V logic), you must check if the Echo pin is 5V tolerant or use a level shifter. Also power the sensor from 5V, not 3.3V, for reliable readings.

5.4.4 Arduino Sketch (Optional)

If you're using an **Arduino** as the microcontroller, you can test the sensor with a simple sketch:

```cpp
cpp

#define TRIG_PIN 9
```

```
#define ECHO_PIN 8

void setup() {
  Serial.begin(9600);
  pinMode(TRIG_PIN, OUTPUT);
  pinMode(ECHO_PIN, INPUT);
}

void loop() {
  digitalWrite(TRIG_PIN, LOW);
  delayMicroseconds(2);
  digitalWrite(TRIG_PIN, HIGH);
  delayMicroseconds(10);
  digitalWrite(TRIG_PIN, LOW);

  unsigned long duration = pulseIn(ECHO_PIN,
HIGH);
  // distance in cm = duration / 58.2 (roughly)
  float distance = duration / 58.2;

  Serial.print("Distance: ");
  Serial.print(distance);
  Serial.println(" cm");

  delay(500);
}
```

- This code triggers the sensor, measures the pulse width, and prints the distance over serial. It's a quick sanity check before hooking up to ROS2.

5.4.5 Integrating with ROS2

Now, suppose you have a **ROS2** setup on your Raspberry Pi or another SBC. You could:

1. **Directly** read the timing using a GPIO library in Python, but it's tricky to get accurate microsecond timing in Linux user space.
2. **Use an Arduino** or other MCU running custom firmware or micro-ROS to measure the pulse. Then, it sends the distance to the Pi via serial, which a **ROS2 node** publishes.

5.4.5.1. Minimal ROS2 Node (Python)

If you decide to measure on the Pi with a library like **pigpio** or **RPi.GPIO** (with caution about real-time accuracy):

```
python

#!/usr/bin/env python3

import rclpy
from rclpy.node import Node
from sensor_msgs.msg import Range
import time
import RPi.GPIO as GPIO
```

```
TRIG_PIN = 23
ECHO_PIN = 24

class UltrasonicNode(Node):
    def __init__(self):
        super().__init__('ultrasonic_node')
        self.pub = self.create_publisher(Range,
'ultrasonic_range', 10)
        GPIO.setmode(GPIO.BCM)
        GPIO.setup(TRIG_PIN, GPIO.OUT)
        GPIO.setup(ECHO_PIN, GPIO.IN)
        self.timer = self.create_timer(0.5,
self.read_distance)
        self.get_logger().info("UltrasonicNode
started.")

    def read_distance(self):
        # Trigger pulse
        GPIO.output(TRIG_PIN, False)
        time.sleep(0.000002)
        GPIO.output(TRIG_PIN, True)
        time.sleep(0.00001)
        GPIO.output(TRIG_PIN, False)

        # Wait for echo start
        while GPIO.input(ECHO_PIN) == 0:
            pulse_start = time.time()
```

```
        # Wait for echo end
        while GPIO.input(ECHO_PIN) == 1:
            pulse_end = time.time()

        pulse_duration = pulse_end - pulse_start
        distance = (pulse_duration * 34300) / 2.0
# in cm

        # Publish as a ROS2 Range message
        msg = Range()
        msg.radiation_type = Range.ULTRASOUND
        msg.field_of_view = 0.1
        msg.min_range = 0.02
        msg.max_range = 4.0
        msg.range = distance / 100.0  # convert
cm to meters

        self.pub.publish(msg)
        self.get_logger().info(f"Distance:
{distance:.2f} cm")

def main(args=None):
    rclpy.init(args=args)
    node = UltrasonicNode()
    try:
        rclpy.spin(node)
    except KeyboardInterrupt:
```

```
        node.get_logger().info("Shutting down 
UltrasonicNode.")
    finally:
        node.destroy_node()
        GPIO.cleanup()
        rclpy.shutdown()


if __name__ == '__main__':
    main()
```

Caution: *The code above depends on the Pi's timing stability. If you need more precise or stable readings, it's recommended to handle the ultrasonic reading logic in a microcontroller and then forward the results to the Pi or SBC. Still, for prototyping, this approach can work.*

5.4.6 Testing

- **Step 1**: Wire the sensor correctly.
- **Step 2**: Install the required Python libraries (sudo apt install python3-rpi.gpio).
- **Step 3**: Run your node: ros2 run ultrasonic_pkg ultrasonic_node.
- **Step 4**: In another terminal, check the data: ros2 topic echo /ultrasonic_range.

You should see the distance update roughly every half-second. Move your hand or an object closer to the sensor to see the distance decrease.

5.5. Real-World Applications: Manufacturing, Healthcare, and Beyond

So, how do these fundamentals—microcontrollers, sensors, communication protocols, and ROS2 integration—translate into **actual industries**?

5.5.1 Manufacturing

- **Assembly Lines**: Robotic arms with servo or stepper motors handle repetitive tasks at high precision. They rely on encoders, limit switches, and machine vision for quality control.
- **Automated Guided Vehicles (AGVs)**: These mobile robots use LiDAR or cameras to navigate warehouses, employing **CAN** or **Ethernet** to communicate with onboard controllers.
- **Predictive Maintenance**: Vibration and temperature sensors track the health of motors or belts, feeding data into ROS2 for real-time analytics.

5.5.2 Healthcare

- **Surgical Robots**: Extremely high precision with real-time haptic feedback. Microcontrollers handle motor control for robotic arms, while SBCs run image-guided navigation.

- **Rehabilitation Devices:** Exoskeletons powered by brushless motors and controlled by embedded systems. IMUs track patient movements, feeding data into a main controller for therapy analytics.
- **Service Robots**: Hospitals deploy robots for carrying supplies, using ultrasonic and LiDAR to avoid collisions in busy hallways.

5.5.3 Logistics and Retail

- **Last-Mile Delivery Robots**: They navigate sidewalks using a fusion of vision, GPS, and wheel encoders. ROS2 orchestrates route planning, while onboard microcontrollers manage motor speeds.
- **Automated Storage and Retrieval Systems (AS/RS)**: Overhead crane-like robots or floor-bound shuttles fetch and store inventory, often using **CAN** for robust, fault-tolerant communication across multiple actuators.
- **In-Store Robots:** Patrol store aisles to check for out-of-stock items or spills, scanning shelves with camera arrays and sending data to a central server.

5.5.4 Agriculture

- **Autonomous Tractors**: Combine GPS, LiDAR, and IMUs to follow pre-defined routes across large fields. Microcontrollers handle hydraulics and engine controls.

- **Smart Greenhouses**: Deploy arrays of temperature, humidity, and pH sensors over **I2C** or wireless protocols, adjusting irrigation or ventilation in real-time.

5.5.5 Exploration and Research

- **Underwater Drones (ROVs)**: Use pressure sensors, sonar, and robust can-bus systems for deep sea exploration.
- **Planetary Rovers**: NASA's Mars rovers rely on radiation-hardened microcontrollers, specialized sensors, and robust data buses to handle extreme conditions.
- **Disaster Response**: Robots with cameras and LiDAR navigate collapsed buildings to find survivors, typically using advanced hardware to detect and map debris.

Conclusion of Chapter 5

We've journeyed through the **hardware landscape** of robotics, from **microcontrollers** and **SBCs** to the **sensors** and **protocols** that keep everything connected. We also looked at an **ultrasonic sensor** project to illustrate how you might wire and read real-time distances via ROS2. Lastly, we explored how these hardware fundamentals enable robots in **manufacturing**, **healthcare**, **logistics**, **agriculture**, and beyond.

Key Takeaways

1. **Hardware Choice**: Microcontrollers handle real-time tasks; SBCs run robust OS platforms (often with ROS2). Many robots combine both to balance performance and complexity.
2. **Sensors & Actuators**: Understanding how each sensor works (ultrasonic, LiDAR, IMU, etc.) is crucial for selecting and integrating them effectively.
3. **Communication Protocols**: UART, SPI, I2C, CAN–each has unique pros and cons. Pick the protocol that suits your speed, distance, and multi-node requirements.
4. **ROS2 Integration**: Whether you run micro-ROS on an MCU or communicate via a serial protocol, bridging hardware data into ROS2 topics is the cornerstone of a flexible, modular robot.
5. **Real-World Impact**: These building blocks aren't just for hobby projects; they power industry-scale solutions from assembly lines to surgical robots.

Frequently Asked Questions

1. **Q**: Can I just use a Raspberry Pi for everything instead of a microcontroller?
   A: For many tasks, yes. However, if you need precise timing or plan to handle multiple fast sensors, a

microcontroller might be better suited—or you can combine both.

2. **Q**: Which microcontroller is best for running micro-ROS?
   A: STM32 boards, ESP32, and some other ARM-based microcontrollers have decent micro-ROS support. Check the official Micro-ROS documentation for compatibility and examples.

3. **Q**: How do I choose between LiDAR, ultrasonic, or infrared distance sensors?
   A: It depends on range, environment, and budget. LiDAR offers a 2D or 3D scan with high accuracy but costs more. Ultrasonic is cheaper, good for shorter distances, and less resolution. Infrared is also short-range and can have issues with certain surfaces.

4. **Q**: I'm building a heavy robot. How do I handle motor power?
   A: You'll likely need separate **motor drivers** or ESCs that accept control signals (PWM or CAN) from a microcontroller or SBC. Make sure your power supply can handle peak current and use fuses or circuit breakers for safety.

5. **Q**: I see references to using Docker with ROS2. Does that affect hardware access?
   A: Docker can be used to containerize your ROS2 environment. For hardware, you'll need to pass through USB or device nodes from the host OS.

While Docker can simplify software deployment, ensure your container has the correct privileges to access /dev/tty devices, GPIO, or other hardware interfaces.

What's Next?

Now that you've seen how hardware and ROS2 fit together, the next chapters will delve deeper into **sensors and perception**, **navigation**, and more advanced aspects like **state machines** and **behavior trees**. As you integrate more sensors—like cameras, IMUs, or LiDAR—your robot's capability to perceive and navigate will skyrocket.

Consider trying additional hands-on experiments:

- **Add a servo** to your ultrasonic sensor, scanning left and right to create a basic 2D map of distances.
- **Integrate** a real LiDAR (e.g., RPLidar) and practice generating a map in ROS2 using SLAM.
- **Experiment** with motor drivers (like L298N or TB6612FNG) to control DC motors, publishing velocity commands from a ROS2 node.

Remember, as you incorporate more hardware, your robot becomes physically and functionally more complex. Stick to best practices—**clean wiring, clear documentation**, and **modular code**—to keep your hardware and software in sync. Welcome to the physical world of robotics, where you'll soon see your robot come to life and begin interacting with its environment in truly exciting ways!

Chapter 6: Sensors and Perception

For a robot to interact intelligently with the world, it must first **perceive** what's happening around it. That's where **sensors** come into play—providing the robot with information about its environment, its orientation, and even the people or objects it might encounter. In this chapter, we'll explore the different types of sensors commonly found in robotics, how to **fuse** the data from multiple sensors, and how to use powerful computer vision tools like **OpenCV** for real-time object detection. We'll also tackle the inevitable challenges—such as noise, calibration, and unpredictable real-world conditions—and outline strategies to overcome them.

By the end of this chapter, you'll have a solid grasp of how to integrate various sensors into a ROS2-based robotics platform, process their data effectively, and apply computer vision techniques for advanced perception tasks. Let's dive in!

6.1. Types of Sensors (Camera, LiDAR, IMU, Infrared, etc.)

Modern robots rely on a **wide array** of sensors for tasks like navigation, object detection, motion control, and more.

Understanding the most commonly used sensor types—and their strengths and weaknesses—will help you select the right tools for your projects.

6.1.1 Cameras

- **Role**: Provide visual information in the form of images or video streams. This is crucial for tasks such as **object recognition**, **visual servoing**, and **scene understanding.**
- **Subtypes:**
    1. **Monocular Cameras**: Standard 2D cameras (e.g., USB webcams).
    2. **Stereo Cameras:** Two-lens systems offering depth perception by comparing the offset between the left and right images.
    3. **Depth Cameras:** (e.g., Intel RealSense, Microsoft Kinect) use infrared or structured light to generate a depth map, enabling 3D perception.
- **Pros**: High information density (colors, shapes, textures).
- **Cons:** Susceptible to lighting changes, reflections, and occlusions. Processing camera data can also be computationally intensive.

Analogy: Think of a camera as the "eyes" of your robot, capturing visual cues that the robot can interpret—just like how humans rely heavily on vision to understand our surroundings.

6.1.2 LiDAR (Light Detection and Ranging)

- **Role:** Uses laser beams to measure distances to objects in the environment, creating a **point cloud** or a **2D/3D scan.**
- **Examples:**
    - **2D LiDAR** (e.g., Hokuyo, RPLIDAR) that spins on a single axis for a flat horizontal scan.
    - **3D LiDAR** (e.g., Velodyne, Ouster) capturing an entire 3D environment by scanning multiple layers simultaneously.
- **Pros:** Very precise distance measurements, good for mapping and navigation. LiDAR is robust in varied lighting conditions.
- **Cons:** Typically more expensive. Some LiDARs have limited range or might struggle with highly reflective or transparent surfaces.

6.1.3 IMU (Inertial Measurement Unit)

- **Composition:** Usually includes an **accelerometer**, **gyroscope**, and sometimes a **magnetometer**.
- **Role:** Measures **orientation**, **acceleration**, and **angular velocity**, which are essential for tasks like **balancing**, **state estimation**, or **navigation**.

- **Pros**: Low-latency data about motion; helps in stabilizing drones, robotic arms, or mobile robots.
- **Cons**: Data can drift over time due to integration errors (the "drift" problem). Usually paired with other sensors (like GPS or wheel encoders) for accuracy.

6.1.4 Infrared and Ultrasonic Rangefinders

- **Infrared (IR) Sensors**: Emit IR light and measure reflections to gauge distance. They're cheap and simple but can be affected by ambient light or reflective surfaces.
- **Ultrasonic Sensors**: Measure the time it takes for ultrasonic pulses to bounce back from an obstacle. They work well for short to medium ranges, often used in obstacle avoidance.

Pros: Affordable, straightforward to interface (e.g., HC-SR04).
Cons: Less resolution or range than LiDAR. They can also have issues with soft or angled surfaces that absorb or deflect signals.

6.1.5 Specialized Sensors

- **GPS (Global Positioning System)**: Useful for outdoor robots that need global positioning.
- **Pressure and Force Sensors**: For robots that need to grip objects gently or walk on uneven terrain.

- **Thermal Cameras:** Detect temperature variations, useful in surveillance or search-and-rescue scenarios.

Overview of Common Robot Sensors

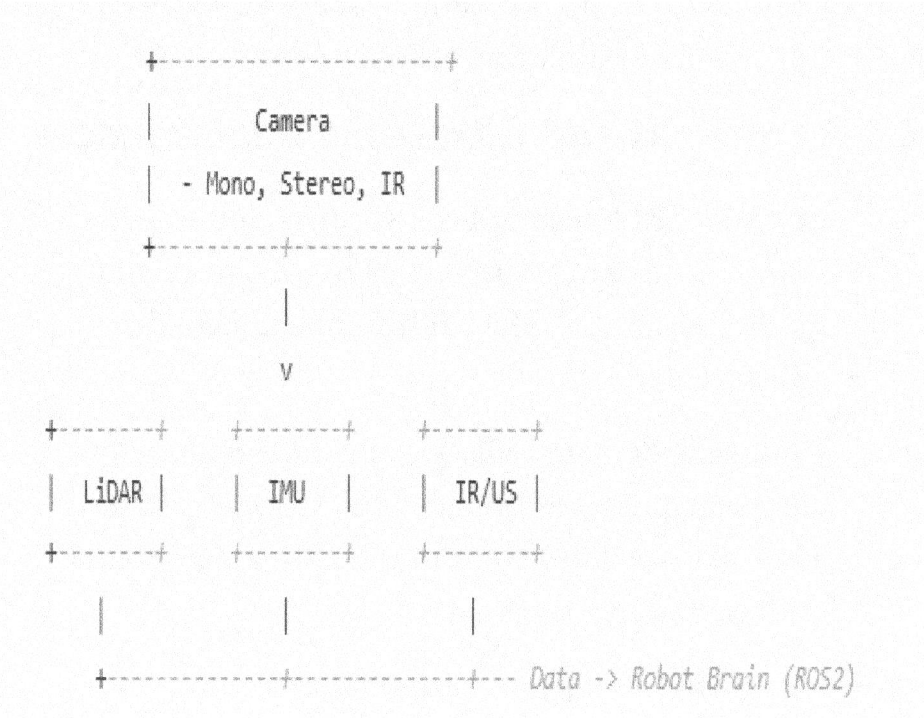

This diagram shows some of the core sensors feeding data into a central ROS2 system.

6.2. Sensor Fusion Concepts and ROS2 Tools

No single sensor can give your robot a perfect view of reality. Instead, real-world systems rely on **sensor fusion**—combining data from multiple sensors to produce a **richer, more accurate** understanding.

6.2.1 Why Sensor Fusion?

1. **Compensating Weaknesses:** A camera might fail in low light, whereas a LiDAR remains unaffected. An IMU might drift, but a GPS can reset global position.
2. **Enhanced Accuracy:** Merging partial readings from multiple sensors can reduce noise and uncertainty, leading to more robust estimates of position or environment.
3. **Redundancy:** If one sensor fails or gives inconsistent data, the system can fall back on others.

6.2.2 Common Sensor Fusion Approaches

1. **Kalman Filters (KF)**: Recursive estimators that fuse noisy sensor data (IMU, wheel encoders, GPS) to get the best possible state estimate.
2. **Extended Kalman Filter (EKF)**: A variant of KF that handles non-linear sensor models (very common in robotics).
3. **Particle Filters:** Used in **SLAM** (Simultaneous Localization and Mapping) or robot localization, especially for complex, non-Gaussian noise distributions.
4. **Deep Learning**: For high-level fusion (e.g., combining camera images with LiDAR data for object detection).

This requires more computational resources but can yield rich semantic understanding.

6.2.3 ROS2 Tools for Sensor Fusion

- **robot_localization:** A popular ROS (and ROS2) package providing EKF and UKF (Unscented Kalman Filter) solutions for state estimation.
- **nav2 stack:** Includes modules for localizing your robot, building maps, and planning paths. Typically fuses odometry, IMU, and LiDAR or camera data.
- **tf2:** ROS2's transform library that keeps track of coordinate frames (e.g., base_link, map, odom). Essential for sensor fusion across different reference frames.

Example Workflow: Your IMU publishes orientation data, your wheel encoders publish odometry, and your LiDAR-based local SLAM node publishes robot pose estimates. A node running robot_localization fuses these inputs to provide a stable, drift-minimized estimate of the robot's pose in the environment.

6.3. OpenCV for Computer Vision in Python

Computer Vision is a pillar of modern robotics, enabling tasks like object detection, facial recognition, scene segmentation, and more. **OpenCV** (Open Source Computer Vision) is the go-to library in Python for many of these functionalities.

6.3.1 Why OpenCV?

1. **Comprehensive:** Offers a massive range of tools for image processing, feature detection, tracking, and more.
2. **Optimized:** Written in C++ under the hood but exposed to Python, giving a balance of speed and usability.
3. **Community:** Large user base, abundant tutorials, and a wealth of ready-made algorithms.

6.3.2 Core Concepts in OpenCV

1. **Reading and Writing Images**

```
python


import cv2
img = cv2.imread("image.jpg")
cv2.imwrite("output.jpg", img)
```

   - Use this for basic file I/O, verifying your camera's output or logging snapshots.

2. **Image Processing**

```
python


gray = cv2.cvtColor(img, cv2.COLOR_BGR2GRAY)
```

```
blurred = cv2.GaussianBlur(gray, (5,5), 0)
edges = cv2.Canny(blurred, 50, 150)
```

- Typical steps include **color conversion, blurring,** and **edge detection.**
- These steps help in highlighting features that are important for your robot's tasks (e.g., boundary of an object).

3. **Feature Detection**

```
python

orb = cv2.ORB_create()
keypoints, descriptors =
orb.detectAndCompute(gray, None)
```

- Detect corners, blobs, or keypoints in an image for tasks like SLAM or object recognition.

4. **Object Detection**

- **Classical methods:** Haar Cascades for face detection, HOG (Histogram of Oriented Gradients) for people detection.
- **Deep Learning:** DNN modules in OpenCV can load and run neural networks like YOLO, TensorFlow, or Caffe models.

6.3.3 Integrating OpenCV with ROS2

1. **Image Transport:** A ROS2 concept for publishing and subscribing to image data (e.g., from a camera driver).

2. **cv_bridge**: Bridges ROS2 Image messages to OpenCV's Mat or numpy arrays in Python, letting you process them easily.
3. **Pipelining**: Typically, you'll have a node that subscribes to a **camera topic**, uses cv_bridge to convert the frames into OpenCV format, performs some processing, and **publishes** the results (or triggers an action if an object is detected).

Example:

```
python


import rclpy
from rclpy.node import Node
from sensor_msgs.msg import Image
from cv_bridge import CvBridge
import cv2


class VisionNode(Node):
    def __init__(self):
        super().__init__('vision_node')
        self.subscription =
self.create_subscription(
            Image,
            'camera/image_raw',
            self.image_callback,
            10
        )
```

```
        self.bridge = CvBridge()

    def image_callback(self, img_msg):
        frame =
self.bridge.imgmsg_to_cv2(img_msg,
desired_encoding='bgr8')
        # Process the frame with OpenCV
        gray = cv2.cvtColor(frame,
cv2.COLOR_BGR2GRAY)
        # ...
        cv2.imshow('Camera View', frame)
        cv2.waitKey(1)

def main(args=None):
    rclpy.init(args=args)
    node = VisionNode()
    rclpy.spin(node)
    node.destroy_node()
    cv2.destroyAllWindows()
    rclpy.shutdown()

if __name__ == '__main__':
    main()
```

Computer Vision Pipeline in ROS2

```
Camera Driver (publish) --> [ Image Msg ] --> Vision Node (subscribe)
                                                   |
                                                   v
                                          cv_bridge Conversion
                                                   |
                                                   v
                                 OpenCV Processing (e.g., object detection)
                                                   |
                                                   v
                                            Robot Actions or
                                        Published "Detected Objects"
```

6.4. Hands-On Project: Real-Time Object Detection with a Camera and OpenCV

Now, let's roll up our sleeves for a **practical** project. We'll grab a camera feed, run a basic **object detection** model (like a YOLO or a Haar Cascade) in real time, and display detection results. This scenario is widely applicable—think of a robot that must avoid obstacles or identify markers to navigate.

6.4.1 Project Overview

1. **Hardware**: A basic USB camera or a Pi camera.
2. **Software**: Python, OpenCV, and a small **deep learning** or classical detection model.
3. **Goal**: Detect a specific object (e.g., a face, a bottle, or a custom YOLO class) and visualize bounding boxes in real time.

6.4.2 Dependencies and Setup

1. **Install OpenCV** (e.g., pip install opencv-python).
2. **Download a Pretrained Model**: For simplicity, let's use a pretrained **Haar Cascade** for face detection. (If you'd like to detect something else, you can find or train your own cascade or YOLO model.)

```bash
# Example for face cascade
wget
https://raw.githubusercontent.com/opencv/opencv/master/data/haarcascades/haarcascade_frontalface_default.xml
```

3. **Project Structure**:

```css
real_time_detection/
├── main.py
```

```
├── haarcascade_frontalface_default.xml
└── requirements.txt
```

6.4.3 main.py

```
python

import cv2
import time

def main():
    # Load the Cascade
    face_cascade =
cv2.CascadeClassifier('haarcascade_frontalface_de
fault.xml')

    # Open a camera stream (0 is default webcam)
    cap = cv2.VideoCapture(0)
    if not cap.isOpened():
        print("Error: Cannot open camera")
        return

    while True:
        ret, frame = cap.read()
        if not ret:
            print("Failed to grab frame")
            break
```

```
        # Convert to grayscale for cascade
detection
        gray = cv2.cvtColor(frame,
cv2.COLOR_BGR2GRAY)

        # Detect faces
        faces =
face_cascade.detectMultiScale(gray,
scaleFactor=1.1, minNeighbors=5, minSize=(30,
30))

        # Draw bounding boxes
        for (x, y, w, h) in faces:
            cv2.rectangle(frame, (x, y), (x+w,
y+h), (0, 255, 0), 2)

        # Show frame
        cv2.imshow("Real-Time Detection", frame)

        # Press 'q' to quit
        if cv2.waitKey(1) & 0xFF == ord('q'):
            break

    cap.release()
    cv2.destroyAllWindows()

if __name__ == "__main__":
    main()
```

Explanation:

1. We load a **Haar Cascade** for face detection.
2. Capture frames from the webcam.
3. Convert each frame to **grayscale** (faster for detection).
4. **Detect** faces and draw rectangles around them.
5. Display results in real-time, exiting on a key press.

6.4.4 Possible Extensions

- **ROS2 Integration:** Wrap this script in a ROS2 node that publishes bounding box coordinates, so other nodes can act on detections.
- **YOLO or DNN:** Replace the Haar Cascade with a **YOLOv5** or **SSD** detection model for more robust multi-object detection.
- **Performance Tweaks:** If you need more speed, leverage **GPU** (CUDA / OpenCL) versions of OpenCV or hardware accelerators (like NVIDIA Jetson's Tensor Cores).

6.5. Challenges and Solutions: Noise, Calibration, and Environmental Factors

In a perfect world, sensor data would always be accurate, stable, and unaffected by external conditions. Reality, however, is messy. Noise, misalignment, or dynamic lighting can degrade sensor readings, leading to errors or failures.

6.5.1 Noise in Sensor Readings

Noise can be due to electronic interference, mechanical vibrations, or environmental variations. For instance, an IMU might pick up motor vibrations, or a camera might see pixel-level noise in low light.

Solutions:

1. **Filtering:**
    - **Low-pass filters** (e.g., moving average, Butterworth) for smoothing out high-frequency noise.
    - **Kalman filters** for robust state estimation in dynamic scenarios.
2. **Hardware Shielding:**
    - Isolate sensitive sensors from motors or use dampening materials to reduce vibrations.

- Properly ground your circuits and use twisted pairs or shielded cables for signals.

3. **Sensor Fusion:**
   - Cross-check or average out conflicting data from multiple sensors to reduce random fluctuations.

6.5.2 Calibration

Many sensors require **calibration** to ensure correct readings. A camera might need a lens calibration to remove distortion; a LiDAR might need angle alignment; an IMU might need offset correction.

1. **Intrinsic Calibration** (for cameras): Correct lens distortion, set focal length, principal point, etc. Tools like camera_calibration in ROS can help.
2. **Extrinsic Calibration:** Align sensors relative to each other or the robot's reference frame (e.g., ensure your camera's coordinate frame matches the robot's base_link in tf2).
3. **Regular Re-Calibration:** Over time, mechanical shifts, temperature changes, or lens movement can degrade a once-accurate calibration.

6.5.3 Environmental Factors

Your robot might encounter:

1. **Lighting Changes:** Direct sunlight, shadows, or artificial lighting can wreak havoc on cameras.

2. **Reflective or Transparent Surfaces:** LiDAR or IR sensors might misinterpret glass or shiny objects.
3. **Weather:** Rain, fog, or dust can scatter laser beams or degrade camera images.
4. **Magnetic Interference:** A magnetometer in an IMU might get thrown off near large metallic structures or electromagnetic fields.

Solutions:

- **Dynamic Parameter Tuning:** Adjust camera exposure, LiDAR detection thresholds, or sensor gains on the fly.
- **Deploy Redundant Sensor Types:** If one fails in a certain condition (e.g., heavy fog for LiDAR), another (e.g., radar) might still work.
- **Environmental Modeling:** Use machine learning or specialized filters to detect and adapt to changing conditions.

6.5.4 Fail-Safes and Redundancy

Critical robots (e.g., surgical or automotive) often incorporate **redundant** sensors. If your primary LiDAR fails, a secondary sensor can keep the system operational or guide it to a safe stop. Designing with failsafes requires thorough testing in varied conditions—both in simulation (e.g., Gazebo) and real-world scenarios.

Common Sensor Challenges

```
+-------------+     +-----------------------+
| Sensor Noise| --> |   Apply filters (KF,MA)  |
+-------------+     +-----------------------+
        |
        v
+---------------+   +-------------------------------+
| Calibration   |--> |  camera_calibration, extrinsics    |
+---------------+   +-------------------------------+
        |
        v
+--------------------+    +----------------------------------------+
| Environmental Issues|-> | dynamic parameters, multi-sensor redundancy |
+--------------------+    +----------------------------------------+
```

This flow chart represents how you might address noise, calibration, and environment factors systematically in your sensor pipeline.

Conclusion of Chapter 6

From **camera-based** perception to **LiDAR** scans, **IMU** orientation data, and the crucial role of **sensor fusion**, we've explored the intricacies of giving robots the ability to sense their environment. We also looked at **OpenCV** for real-time vision tasks, culminating in a hands-on project that showcases object detection. Lastly, we delved into potential pitfalls—noise, calibration, changing environments—and how to mitigate them.

Key Takeaways

1. **Sensor Diversity:** Each sensor type (cameras, LiDAR, IMUs, etc.) has unique advantages and limitations. Combining them offers broader coverage and redundancy.
2. **Sensor Fusion**: Tools like **Kalman filters**, **robot_localization**, and **tf2** in ROS2 help you merge data into a coherent, reliable picture.
3. **OpenCV for CV**: A versatile, powerful library for everything from simple edge detection to advanced neural network inference, essential for advanced robotics.
4. **Real-Time Object Detection**: Combining a camera feed with OpenCV transforms your robot into a platform that can identify and act upon objects in its environment.
5. **Robustness**: Combat sensor noise, calibration drift, and environmental variations through thorough testing, filtering, and system design.

Frequently Asked Questions

1. **Q**: Which sensor is best for both indoor and outdoor navigation?
   A: LiDAR often excels in structured indoor environments, but for outdoor conditions, you might

need a combination of LiDAR, GPS, and camera, depending on range, lighting, and budget.

2. **Q**: How do I handle camera lag or high CPU usage?
   A: Explore hardware acceleration (GPU or specialized coprocessors), reduce frame resolution, or offload heavy computation to a more powerful onboard or cloud-based system.

3. **Q**: Do I need advanced math to implement sensor fusion?
   A: A conceptual grasp of state estimation and filtering is helpful. However, ROS2 packages like robot_localization abstract many details, letting you configure filters rather than writing them from scratch.

4. **Q**: How do I calibrate a multi-camera setup for stereo vision?
   A: Use stereo calibration tools (e.g., OpenCV's stereoCalibrate) or ROS calibration packages. You'll need a calibration pattern and careful setup.

5. **Q**: Can I run deep learning models on a Raspberry Pi for object detection?
   A: Yes, but performance may be limited. Consider hardware accelerators like the Intel Movidius Neural Compute Stick or an NVIDIA Jetson if you need higher FPS.

What's Next?

We've now built a **strong foundation** in robotics perception. Next, we'll look at how to use this sensor data for **navigation**, planning paths, and ensuring robots move intelligently. Whether you're building a mobile robot that must avoid obstacles or a robotic arm that picks objects from a conveyor belt, these perception techniques—and the knowledge of sensor integration—form the backbone of advanced robotics.

Up Next: Navigation and Path Planning—where we combine sensor data with motion planning algorithms, giving your robot the autonomy to explore and interact with the world confidently.

Chapter 7: Robot Navigation and Path Planning

So, you've wired up your sensors, integrated them with ROS2, and even gotten a handle on computer vision. Now the real fun begins—giving your robot the **ability to move** in a purposeful, autonomous manner. Robot navigation is not just about motors and wheels; it's about **understanding the environment**, **figuring out where to go**, and **planning a safe route** to get there. In this chapter, we'll break down the fundamentals of **robot kinematics** (to ensure we know how wheels and steering actually work), then dive into the powerful **ROS2 Navigation Stack (Nav2)**, explore **SLAM** (Simultaneous Localization and Mapping), and end with a **hands-on project** that ties everything together. We'll also include tips and tricks for **tuning** your navigation parameters so that your robot moves smoothly and reliably in real-world scenarios.

By the end, you'll have a **strong grasp** on how to design, set up, and troubleshoot a navigation system for your mobile robot—whether it's a small differential-drive platform or a full-sized Ackermann-steered rover.

7.1. The Basics of Robot Kinematics (Differential Drive, Ackermann Steering)

When we talk about **navigation and path planning**, we're not just dealing with software. We need to understand the **physical constraints** of how a robot actually moves. A mismatch between your chosen control model and the real mechanical behavior of your robot can lead to poor or completely failed navigation.

7.1.1 Differential Drive Kinematics

Differential drive is one of the most common configurations for mobile robots—think two powered wheels on a shared axis and possibly a caster wheel for balance. Each wheel can spin independently in forward or reverse, which lets the robot:

1. **Move Straight** if both wheels rotate at the same speed and direction.
2. **Turn in Place** if one wheel goes forward while the other goes backward at the same speed.
3. **Arc Turn** if they spin at different speeds.

Key Kinematic Equations (simplified):

- Let vLv_LvL be the linear velocity of the left wheel and vRv_RvR be the velocity of the right wheel.

- The **linear velocity** vvv of the robot's center is roughly the average:

$$v = \frac{v_L + v_R}{2}.$$

- The **angular velocity** ω\omegaω (about the center of the axle) is proportional to the difference:

$$\omega = \frac{v_R - v_L}{d},$$

, where d is the distance between the two wheels.

Advantages:

- Simple mechanics—just two motors and a pivot.
- Excellent maneuverability, including on-the-spot rotations.

Challenges:

- Slippage can occur if the robot starts or stops quickly, or on slippery floors.
- Odometry can drift over time due to wheel slip or uneven terrain.

7.1.2 Ackermann Steering Kinematics

Ackermann steering is what you see in most automobiles. The front wheels turn at different angles to allow the vehicle to follow a curved path without tire scrubbing. In robotics, you might see **Ackermann** setups for car-like robots or outdoor rovers.

Basics:

- Only the front wheels typically steer.
- The rear wheels are driven, or sometimes all four wheels can be powered.
- **Turning Radius** is derived from the geometry of how the front wheels pivot around a common center point that extends from the rear axle.

Key Equations (simplified):

- Suppose you have a wheelbase LLL (distance between front and rear axles).
- If the front wheels steer at an angle δ\deltaδ, the robot's turning radius RRR from the center of the rear axle is approximately:

$$R = \frac{L}{\tan(\delta)}.$$

- The robot's angular velocity ω\omegaω around that center point is:

$$\omega = \frac{v}{R},$$

, where vvv is the linear speed of the robot.

Advantages:

- Minimizes tire wear and skidding on roads or rough surfaces.
- Ideal for higher speeds (like an autonomous car or outdoor rover).

Challenges:

- Requires more complex steering mechanisms.
- The navigation stack must account for the limited turning radius and not assume you can spin in place.

Differential Drive vs. Ackermann Steering

```
(Differential Drive)                    (Ackermann Steering)
     <--- d --->
   L O          O R                 O--------O
                                   /          \
           ^                      |            |
   Robot   |                      |  Car-Like  |
   Center  |                      \           /
                                   O--------O
```

This diagram highlights the difference in wheel layouts. Differential drive wheels can rotate independently in place, whereas Ackermann steering has front wheels turning about a pivot.

7.2. ROS2 Navigation Stack Overview (Nav2)

ROS2's **Navigation2** (often abbreviated as **Nav2**) is a suite of packages that help you turn high-level goals (like "Go to X, Y location in the map") into low-level motor commands. Nav2 is the successor to the ROS1 Navigation Stack, re-architected for ROS2's modern features, like DDS-based communication and improved modularity.

7.2.1 Nav2 Components

1. **SLAM / Localization:** Feeds the robot's pose estimate to the navigation stack.
2. **Map Server:** Loads or serves a map of the environment (either 2D occupancy grids or other representations).
3. **Planner:** Computes the path from the robot's current pose to the goal.
4. **Controller:** Generates velocity commands (twist messages) to follow the planned path in real-time, avoiding obstacles.
5. **Recovery Behaviors:** Actions taken if the robot gets stuck (e.g., rotating in place or backing up).
6. **Lifecycle Management:** Nav2 nodes are managed via a lifecycle approach, ensuring each stage of operation (unconfigured, inactive, active, finalized) is handled systematically.

7.2.2 Typical Data Flow in Nav2

1. A **Localization** node (e.g., AMCL or SLAM) publishes the robot's current pose.
2. The **Map Server** provides a static or dynamically updated map to the **Planner**.
3. You send a **navigation goal** (a 2D pose) via an action server.

4. The **Planner** returns a global path.
5. The **Controller** tracks the path locally, taking sensor data (e.g., LiDAR) into account for obstacle avoidance.
6. The **robot** moves step by step, updating its position and continuing until it reaches the goal or an error occurs.

7.2.3 Common Nav2 Nodes

- **nav2_map_server**: Provides the map.
- **nav2_planner**: Global path planner (e.g., Dijkstra-based or A* variants).
- **nav2_controller**: Local path follower (e.g., DWB controller, Teb local planner).
- **nav2_behavior_tree**: Orchestrates overall navigation logic using a behavior tree approach.
- **nav2_bt_navigator**: High-level node sending goals and transitions states.

Diagram 7.2: Nav2 High-Level Architecture

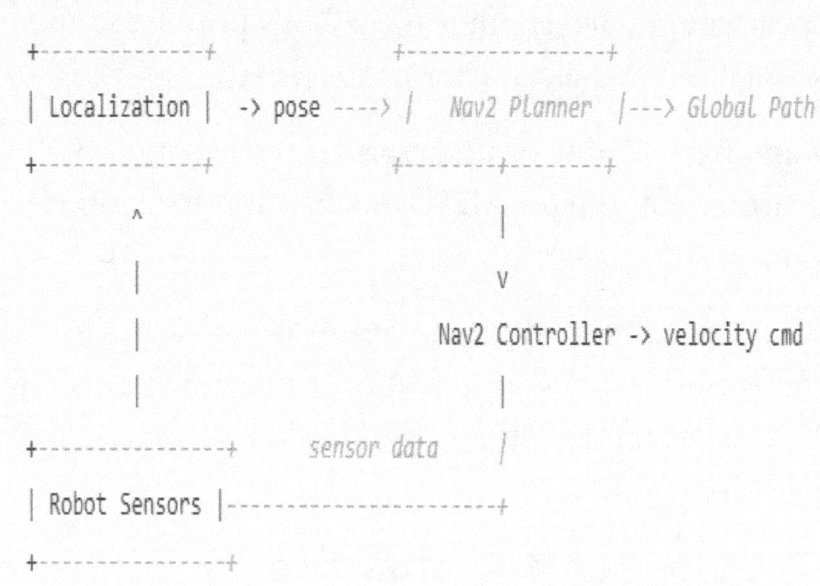

In this simplified diagram, the localization node feeds the current pose, the planner computes the route, and the controller issues velocity commands to the robot.

7.3. SLAM (Simultaneous Localization and Mapping) Fundamentals

SLAM is the process by which a robot **builds a map** of an unknown environment while simultaneously **locating itself** within that map. It's a game-changer for robots operating in new or dynamic spaces—think warehouse robots that need to adapt to changing layouts or consumer robots that learn your home's floor plan.

7.3.1 Core Principles

1. **Localization:** Determining the robot's pose (x, y, and orientation) in a given coordinate system.
2. **Mapping:** Creating or updating a representation of the environment (often a 2D occupancy grid for indoor robots).
3. **Data Association:** Matching sensor observations to previously recorded map features. This is where many SLAM algorithms differ (scan matching, feature-based matching, etc.).

7.3.2 Popular SLAM Approaches

- **GMapping** (ROS1 classic, but ported or replaced by newer options in ROS2).
- **hector_slam** (uses LiDAR data directly, good for small indoor drones).
- **Cartographer** (by Google, robust for 2D, has 3D capabilities).
- **SLAM Toolbox** (a popular choice in ROS2, flexible, good for lifelong mapping).

Each approach has tradeoffs in terms of **compute cost, sensor type** (LiDAR vs. camera vs. depth sensor), and environment types (indoor corridors vs. large open spaces).

7.3.3 Why SLAM Matters

1. **Unknown Environments**: If no prior map is available, the robot can't just localize itself with standard techniques like AMCL. SLAM is required.
2. **Dynamic or Changing Environments**: The map might need real-time updates if obstacles move or the layout changes.
3. **Research & Beyond**: SLAM is a hot topic in robotics research, fueling technologies like self-driving cars (some modules rely on advanced SLAM variants) or augmented reality.

7.4. Hands-On Project: Setting Up a Mobile Robot with Nav2 for Autonomous Navigation

Now for the exciting part–getting your robot to roam around autonomously using the **ROS2 Navigation Stack**. This project assumes you have a **mobile robot** (real or simulated) equipped with:

- A LiDAR or depth camera for obstacle detection.
- Wheel encoders or some mechanism for odometry.
- A microcontroller or direct SBC-based motor control.

- A way to run ROS2 (e.g., Raspberry Pi, Jetson Nano, or PC).

If you're lacking a physical robot, you can simulate one using **Gazebo** or **Ignition** with a supported robot model.

7.4.1 Step 1: Prepare Your Robot Description & URDF

1. **URDF (Unified Robot Description Format)**: Contains your robot's geometry, joints, sensors, etc.
2. Make sure your URDF or xacro file includes the LiDAR plugin or camera link.
3. You can test your URDF in **RViz** to confirm it loads properly.

Tip: For a simple differential-drive robot, set up the URDF with a base_link, left_wheel, and right_wheel. Define transmissions for controlling the wheels.

7.4.2 Step 2: Install Nav2 Packages

On your ROS2 system, install **Nav2**. For example:

```bash
sudo apt update
sudo apt install ros-<distro>-nav2-bringup
```

Replace <distro> with your ROS2 distribution (e.g., humble, iron).

7.4.3 Step 3: Create a Navigation Launch File

Inside your ROS2 workspace (ros2_ws), create a package named my_robot_nav. Within my_robot_nav/launch, create nav_bringup.launch.py:

```
python

from launch import LaunchDescription
from launch_ros.actions import Node

def generate_launch_description():
    # Example usage of the nav2_bringup package
    nav2_params = '/path/to/nav2_params.yaml'
    map_file = '/path/to/map.yaml'  # if you have
a static map

    return LaunchDescription([
        Node(
            package='nav2_bringup',
            executable='bringup_launch.py',
            output='screen',
            parameters=[nav2_params],
            arguments=['--map', map_file]
        ),
    ])
```

7.4.4 Step 4: Configure Nav2 Parameters

Create a nav2_params.yaml file:

```
yaml

amcl:
  ros__parameters:
    use_map_topic: true
    scan_topic: /scan
    min_particle_cloud_size: 100
    max_particle_cloud_size: 2000
    # ...

bt_navigator:
  ros__parameters:
    default_bt_xml_filename:
"navigate_w_replanning_and_recovery.xml"

controller_server:
  ros__parameters:
    controller_plugins: ["FollowPath"]
    # ...
```

This YAML configures each Nav2 module, from **AMCL** (Adaptive Monte Carlo Localization) to the **behavior tree** for navigation. Adjust them based on your sensors and environment.

7.4.5 Step 5: Verify tf2 Transforms and Sensor Topics

- Confirm your robot publishes **odom → base_link** transforms.
- The LiDAR or camera should publish on **/scan** or **/camera/depth**, respectively.
- ros2 topic list and ros2 tf list can help you verify everything is named correctly.

7.4.6 Step 6: Launch and Test

1. Bring up your robot hardware or simulation.
2. Launch your URDF or robot state publisher.
3. Launch nav_bringup.launch.py from your my_robot_nav package:

```
bash

ros2 launch my_robot_nav nav_bringup.launch.py
```

4. Open **RViz**:

```
bash

ros2 launch nav2_bringup rviz_launch.py
```

5. Load the same map or let SLAM run if you have no pre-made map.

6. Set an **initial pose** in RViz (if using AMCL).
7. **Send a navigation goal** by clicking the "2D Nav Goal" button in RViz and selecting a location.
8. Watch your robot plan a path and move. If everything's correct, it should avoid obstacles and reach the goal.

Diagram 7.3: Nav2 Workflow in RViz

```
RViz UI:
  [ Map Display ]
  [ Robot Model ]
  [ 2D Nav Goal Button ]
          |
          v
Nav2 Node (Planner + Controller) -> Robot (publishes velocity)
          ^
          |
Sensors / Pose / Odometry
```

7.4.7 Step 7: Troubleshooting Common Issues

- **Robot spins in circles**: Check that your odometry directions and transforms are correct. A reversed wheel direction can cause chaotic behavior.
- **Local Planner keeps oscillating**: Tweak local planner parameters (e.g., inflation radius for obstacles, path tolerance).
- **Robot collides with obstacles**: Ensure your costmap is receiving the correct sensor data and that your inflation layer is set up properly.

7.5. Tuning and Troubleshooting Navigation: Real-World Tips

Even after setting up Nav2 or a similar navigation framework, real-world operations can bring new surprises. Here's how to **fine-tune** your system and **avoid common pitfalls**.

7.5.1 Tuning Controllers and Planners

1. **Local Planner Gains**:
    - If your robot overshoots corners or wobbles, you might need to reduce the proportional gains or increase the damping.

- Check parameters like max_vel_x, min_vel_x, acc_lim_x or angular equivalents for rotational control.

2. **Costmap Settings:**
   - Increase the **inflation radius** around obstacles if the robot is physically larger or you're worried about collision margin.
   - Adjust the **resolution** of the costmap to balance performance and accuracy. Fine grids can lead to heavier CPU usage.

3. **Global Planner:**
   - If your paths are too close to walls, raise the **cost scaling factor** so the planner avoids edges more aggressively.
   - If the path is too convoluted, you might reduce obstacle_cost_scale or try a different global planner plugin.

7.5.2 Handling Sensor Noise and Drift

1. **Better Odometry:** If wheel slip or sensor drift is high, consider fusing IMU data to stabilize your pose estimates.

2. **Periodic Recalibration:** If you see consistent offsets, re-check your wheel circumference or calibrate your LiDAR.

3. **Filter Data:** You can apply a temporal filter or average scans if you get noisy distance readings.

7.5.3 Recovery Behaviors

When the robot gets stuck, Nav2 can **perform recovery actions** like spinning in place or clearing costmaps. Make sure these behaviors are properly configured:

- **Spin:** The robot rotates 360° in place to see if it can find a new path.
- **Backup:** The robot reverses slightly to escape a corner or tight area.
- **Clear Costmap:** If false obstacles get stuck in the map (e.g., dynamic objects that moved on but left a trace in the costmap), clearing can help.

Tip: Overly frequent recovery behaviors can become frustrating. Tune them so your robot tries to navigate first and only triggers recoveries when truly stuck.

7.5.4 Environmental Considerations

- **Indoor Clutter:** If your environment has many moving objects (people, furniture), use a local planner that handles dynamic obstacles well.
- **Outdoor Terrain:** Uneven ground or slopes can affect odometry. Consider IMU-based tilt compensation and a robust chassis design.

- **Reflective Surfaces:** A LiDAR might get odd readings off glass or mirrors, requiring special caution or alternate sensors (like depth cameras or radar).

7.5.5 Data Visualization and Debugging Tools

1. **RViz:** The Swiss army knife for visualizing maps, robot pose, costmaps, and sensor data.
2. **rqt_graph:** Explore nodes and topic connections if something doesn't appear to be hooking up properly.
3. **ros2 topic echo** and **ros2 topic bw:** Inspect topic data or bandwidth usage.
4. **ros2 bag:** Record data for offline analysis. Then replay sensor data to systematically debug navigation issues without driving the robot around repeatedly.

Conclusion of Chapter 7

We've traveled through the **essentials of navigation**—from the kinematics that dictate how a robot moves (differential drive vs. Ackermann) to the powerful **ROS2 Navigation Stack** that orchestrates everything from mapping to path planning and low-level velocity commands. We also peeked into **SLAM** fundamentals for building a map on the fly. Finally, our hands-on project walked us through setting up

Nav2 for an autonomous mobile robot, followed by real-world tuning techniques.

Key Takeaways

1. **Kinematic Models**: Understand your robot's physical movement constraints. Failing to do so leads to inaccurate odometry and poor path-following.
2. **Nav2 Stack**: Provides a flexible, modular approach to mapping, localization, planning, and control—empowering your robot to move autonomously.
3. **SLAM**: Essential for unknown environments. Tools like SLAM Toolbox or Cartographer help your robot build a map while localizing itself.
4. **Hands-On Setup**: Creating a proper URDF, configuring transforms and sensor data, and setting Nav2 parameters is the recipe for success.
5. **Tuning & Troubleshooting**: Navigation is rarely perfect on the first try; dial in parameters, manage sensor noise, and implement robust recovery behaviors.

Frequently Asked Questions

1. **Q**: Do I need a LiDAR for reliable Nav2 usage?
   A: Nav2 works with various sensor inputs—LiDAR is popular, but depth cameras or even 2D cameras with a visual SLAM solution can be used. Reliability depends on the sensor's coverage and accuracy.

2. **Q**: Can I use Nav2 with Ackermann steering?
   A: Yes, but you must ensure your odometry and local planner reflect the nonholonomic constraints (no in-place rotation). You might need a specialized local planner that handles Ackermann kinematics.
3. **Q**: Which SLAM method is best for large indoor spaces?
   A: SLAM Toolbox or **Cartographer** are both good picks for large environments. The final choice often depends on CPU constraints, sensor types, and community support.
4. **Q**: Is 3D navigation in Nav2 supported?
   A: Nav2's primary focus is 2D plane navigation (x-y plane plus orientation). Some packages experiment with 3D, but they are still evolving. 3D navigation requires a more complex representation of the world and different planners.
5. **Q**: My robot drifts over time. Should I rely solely on SLAM?
   A: If you're in a known environment, it might be best to create a solid map once and use AMCL for localization. If it's unknown or dynamic, SLAM is crucial, but adding an IMU or wheel encoders can reduce drift through sensor fusion.

What's Next?

With navigation under your belt, you might look into:

- **Behavior Trees and State Machines:** Orchestrating complex tasks that go beyond just "Drive to Point A."
- **Multi-Robot Coordination:** Coordinating multiple robots to share a map, avoid collisions, and collaborate on tasks.
- **Advanced AI:** Integrating deep learning for dynamic obstacle avoidance, object tracking, or predicting pedestrian movement.

Regardless of your direction, **mastering navigation** is a giant leap toward building fully autonomous robots. Use these foundations, keep iterating, and soon you'll have a robot that can confidently navigate the real world—zigzagging between couches, crossing busy labs, or roaming factory floors to deliver goods.

Chapter 8: State Machines and Behavior Trees

A robot that can navigate, sense, and interact with its surroundings is only part of the story. True intelligence emerges when a robot orchestrates these capabilities in **complex, context-aware behaviors.** In real-world robotics, you can't simply write a single script that handles every situation without quickly facing **spaghetti code**—tangled logic that's nearly impossible to debug or extend. Instead, many developers use **finite state machines** or **behavior trees** to break down tasks into manageable steps or states.

In this chapter, we'll explore:

1. **Managing Complex Robot Behaviors**: Why we need structured approaches like state machines and behavior trees.
2. **Python Tools for Finite State Machines**: Focusing on libraries like smach and py_trees_ros that make it easier to implement robust control logic in Python.
3. **Hands-On Project**: Building a "Delivery Robot" behavior tree that captures how a robot might pick an item, navigate to a drop-off location, and handle unexpected obstacles or errors.

4. **Error Recovery and Robustness:** Practical strategies for ensuring your high-level behavior logic can recover from real-world hiccups.

By the end, you'll understand how to structure **higher-level robot behaviors** using proven design patterns, empowering your robot to handle tasks methodically, adapt to new conditions, and gracefully recover from errors.

8.1. Managing Complex Robot Behaviors

Picture a mobile robot in a warehouse. It needs to pick up objects from different stations, avoid collisions, run diagnostics, handle battery checks, and communicate with a central server. Each of these tasks involves a sequence of **subtasks** and conditions. If we wrote a single monolithic script, the code would quickly become unmanageable.

8.1.1 The Complexity Challenge

- **Conditional Logic Overload:** A simple "if-else" approach can rapidly explode into dozens or hundreds of conditions to handle every scenario.
- **Parallel and Sequential Tasks:** A robot might need to monitor battery levels while simultaneously navigating.
- **Error Handling:** Real-world robotics is unpredictable—sensors can fail, motors might stall, or you might

detect an obstacle mid-route. Where do you handle these exceptions?

8.1.2 Finite State Machines (FSMs)

One popular approach to structuring such logic is with a **finite state machine.** You define **states** that represent distinct modes or phases of operation (e.g., "Navigating," "Picking Up Item," "Delivering"). **Transitions** define how the robot moves from one state to another based on **events** or **conditions** (e.g., "Arrived at pickup location," "Item secured").

Key Advantages:

1. **Clarity:** States and transitions are explicit, so you can see how the robot flows from one behavior to the next.
2. **Modularity:** Each state can encapsulate a particular behavior, making it simpler to test or replace.
3. **Predictability:** You know precisely which transitions are possible from each state.

Potential Drawbacks:

- For highly branching logic or parallel tasks, FSMs can become cumbersome.
- Transition conditions might lead to a large number of states for complex tasks.

8.1.3 Behavior Trees (BTs)

Behavior trees emerged in the gaming industry but have since become popular in robotics because they allow for **hierarchical** and **reactive** behavior design. Instead of focusing solely on states and transitions, behavior trees organize tasks into a tree structure with **nodes** representing actions or decisions. Special **control flow nodes** (like sequences, selectors, or parallels) define how the tree executes child nodes.

Key Advantages:

1. **Scalability:** BTs handle complex branching more gracefully.
2. **Reactivity:** The tree can quickly re-evaluate certain branches if conditions change.
3. **Modularity and Reusability:** You can nest subtrees for repeated behaviors, and each node can be tested in isolation.

Potential Drawbacks:

- Requires a mental shift if you're used to classic FSMs.
- Extra tooling or libraries are needed to handle concurrency or data flow between nodes effectively.

FSM vs. Behavior Tree Comparison

```
+-----------+         +-----------------+
| FSM:      |         | Behavior Tree:  |
| States    |         | Hierarchical    |
| +-----+   |         |  Nodes & Control |
| |Idle |---------------->|  Flow Structures |
| +-----+   |         +-----------------+
| +-----+   |
| |Nav  |   |
| +-----+   |
| +-----+   |
| |Pick |   |
| +-----+   |
+-----------+
```

In an FSM, you have distinct states and transitions. In a BT, you build up tasks in a tree with branches for different behaviors and conditions.

8.2. Python Tools for Finite State Machines (smach, py_trees_ros)

If you're working in a **ROS2 + Python** environment, two noteworthy libraries are **smach** (classic but still used in various forms) and **py_trees_ros**. Let's look at each.

8.2.1 smach: A Classic FSM Library

Originally popularized in ROS1, smach helps define hierarchical state machines in Python. While official ROS2 support has evolved, many of the concepts remain useful.

How it Works:

1. **State Classes:** You create Python classes representing states, each with an execute() method.
2. **Outcomes:** Each state returns an outcome string (e.g., 'succeeded', 'aborted') indicating which transition to follow.
3. **State Machine Assembly:** You assemble a StateMachine or a Concurrence container in code, hooking states together with transitions.

Example Usage (condensed):

```
python

import smach

class MoveBaseState(smach.State):
    def __init__(self):
        smach.State.__init__(self,
outcomes=['success','fail'])

    def execute(self, userdata):
        # Perform navigation
```

```
        result = move_base_to_goal(...)
        if result:
            return 'success'
        else:
            return 'fail'

sm = smach.StateMachine(outcomes=['DONE'])
with sm:
    smach.StateMachine.add('NAV',
MoveBaseState(),

transitions={'success': 'DONE',
                                            'fail':
'NAV'})
```

Pros: Straightforward if you think in terms of states and transitions.
Cons: Handling parallel tasks or partial reactivity can get complicated.

8.2.2 py_trees_ros: A Behavior Tree Approach

py_trees_ros is a Python library that integrates **behavior trees** with ROS (and by extension, ROS2 in many forks or updated versions).

Key Concepts:

1. **Behavior Tree Nodes:** Basic building blocks that do something (Action, Condition, Decorator, etc.).
2. **Composite Nodes**: Control flow types like Selector, Sequence, or Parallel.
3. **Blackboard**: A shared memory space for nodes to read/write data (e.g., current pose, task goals).

Example:

```
python


import py_trees
import py_trees_ros


class
NavigateAction(py_trees.behaviours.Behaviour):
    def __init__(self, name="Navigate"):
        super().__init__(name)
        self.blackboard =
self.attach_blackboard_client(name)

self.blackboard.register_key(key="target_pose",
access=py_trees.common.Access.READ)

    def update(self):
        # Example navigation code
```

```
        result =
move_to_pose(self.blackboard.target_pose)
        if result == 'running':
            return py_trees.common.Status.RUNNING
        elif result == 'done':
            return py_trees.common.Status.SUCCESS
        else:
            return py_trees.common.Status.FAILURE


root =
py_trees.composites.Selector(name="RobotHighLevel
")
sequence =
py_trees.composites.Sequence(name="DeliverySequen
ce")
navigate_node = NavigateAction()
sequence.add_children([navigate_node])
root.add_child(sequence)
```

Pros:

- Great for building and visualizing complex logic.
- Reactive structure can adapt quickly when conditions change.

Cons:

- Learning curve if you're new to BTs.
- Might require additional libraries or bridging to achieve concurrency or advanced data flow.

8.3. Hands-On Project: Building a Delivery Robot Behavior Tree

Let's stitch these concepts together in a concrete example. Imagine a **delivery robot** in a hospital or office building. Its tasks:

1. **Wait for an Order**: A request arrives from a user specifying a pickup location and drop-off location.
2. **Navigate to Pickup**: Robot travels to the pickup area.
3. **Pick Up Item**: Robot might need to position itself or actuate a small arm.
4. **Navigate to Drop-Off**: Moves to the destination.
5. **Drop Off Item**: Places the item and notifies the user.
6. **Return to Idle**: Wait for the next task.

Using a **behavior tree**, we can structure these steps so that the robot can easily handle changes (like new orders or obstacles) without rewriting every piece of logic.

8.3.1 Setting Up the Project

Folder Structure (example):

```
arduino

delivery_robot_bt/
├── package.xml
```

```
├── setup.py
├── delivery_robot_bt
│   ├── __init__.py
│   ├── main_bt.py
│   ├── behaviors.py
│   └── blackboard.py
└── launch
    └── delivery_bt_launch.py
```

1. **package.xml** / **setup.py:** Standard ROS2 Python package structure.
2. **main_bt.py:** Our main entry point, building and executing the behavior tree.
3. **behaviors.py:** Contains custom behavior nodes for tasks like navigation, pickup, drop-off.
4. **blackboard.py:** Could store shared data, like the current order details.

8.3.2 Creating Custom Behavior Nodes

Let's define some simplified nodes using py_trees.

8.3.2.1. WaitForOrder Node

```
python

import py_trees

class WaitForOrder(py_trees.behaviour.Behaviour):
```

```
    def __init__(self, name="WaitForOrder"):
        super().__init__(name)
        self.blackboard =
self.attach_blackboard_client(name)
        self.blackboard.register_key(key="order",
access=py_trees.common.Access.WRITE)

    def initialise(self):
        self.logger.debug(f"[{self.name}] Waiting
for an order...")

    def update(self):
        # In a real scenario, you'd subscribe to
a topic or check a service
        # Simulate receiving an order after some
condition
        new_order = check_for_new_order()
        if new_order:
            self.blackboard.order = new_order
            self.logger.info("Order received!")
            return py_trees.common.Status.SUCCESS
        else:
            return py_trees.common.Status.RUNNING
```

Explanation:

- This node remains in RUNNING state until an order is found.

- Once an order is received, it writes the data to the blackboard and returns SUCCESS.

8.3.2.2. NavigateToLocation Node

```python
class
NavigateToLocation(py_trees.behaviour.Behaviour):
    def __init__(self, name="NavigateToLocation",
location_key="pickup_location"):
        super().__init__(name)
        self.blackboard =
self.attach_blackboard_client(name)

self.blackboard.register_key(key=location_key,
access=py_trees.common.Access.READ)
        self.location_key = location_key

    def initialise(self):
        self.logger.debug(f"[{self.name}]
Initialize navigation to {self.location_key}")
        self.target_location =
getattr(self.blackboard, self.location_key, None)
        if not self.target_location:
            self.logger.error("No target location
found on blackboard!")
            self.feedback_message = "Navigation
aborted: no location"
```

```
            return

    def update(self):
        if not self.target_location:
            return py_trees.common.Status.FAILURE

        nav_result =
navigate_to(self.target_location)
        if nav_result == "running":
            return py_trees.common.Status.RUNNING
        elif nav_result == "arrived":
            return py_trees.common.Status.SUCCESS
```

else:

return py_trees.common.Status.FAILURE

Explanation:

- This node reads a location from the blackboard (pickup_location or dropoff_location) and calls some navigation function.
- Status updates: RUNNING while in transit, SUCCESS on arrival, FAILURE if something goes wrong.

8.3.2.3. PickupItem and DropOffItem Nodes

```
python

class PickupItem(py_trees.behaviour.Behaviour):
    def update(self):
```

```
        # Trigger a manipulator or physical
action
        pickup_result = attempt_pickup()
        if pickup_result == "done":
            return py_trees.common.Status.SUCCESS
        elif pickup_result == "error":
            return py_trees.common.Status.FAILURE
        else:
            return py_trees.common.Status.RUNNING

class DropOffItem(py_trees.behaviour.Behaviour):
    def update(self):
        drop_result = attempt_dropoff()
        if drop_result == "done":
            return py_trees.common.Status.SUCCESS
        elif drop_result == "error":
            return py_trees.common.Status.FAILURE
        else:
            return py_trees.common.Status.RUNNING
```

Explanation:

- These actions might involve controlling a gripper, verifying item pickup with sensors, etc.
- They return RUNNING if still in progress, SUCCESS if completed, or FAILURE if an error occurs.

8.3.3 Composing the Behavior Tree

main_bt.py:

```python
python


import py_trees
import py_trees_ros
from delivery_robot_bt.behaviors import
WaitForOrder, NavigateToLocation, PickupItem,
DropOffItem


def create_delivery_tree():
    root =
py_trees.composites.Selector(name="DeliveryRoot")


    # 1) Wait for a new order
    wait_order_node = WaitForOrder()


    # 2) Sequence for fulfilling the order
    fulfill_sequence =
py_trees.composites.Sequence(name="FulfillOrder")


    # a) Navigate to pickup
    goto_pickup =
NavigateToLocation(name="GotoPickup",
location_key="pickup_location")


    # b) Pickup item
```

```
    pickup_item = PickupItem(name="PickupItem")

    # c) Navigate to drop-off
    goto_dropoff =
NavigateToLocation(name="GotoDropoff",
location_key="dropoff_location")

    # d) Drop off item
    drop_item = DropOffItem(name="DropItem")

    # Add child nodes in order
    fulfill_sequence.add_children([goto_pickup,
pickup_item, goto_dropoff, drop_item])

    # The high-level structure is a Selector
with:
    #   - WaitForOrder
    #   - FulfillOrder (Sequence)
    # If waiting for order fails or doesn't
succeed, it remains in WaitForOrder.
    # Once WaitForOrder is success, the sequence
runs.
    root.add_children([wait_order_node,
fulfill_sequence])

    return root

def main():
```

```
    root = create_delivery_tree()
    behaviour_tree =
py_trees_ros.trees.BehaviourTree(root=root)
    behaviour_tree.setup(timeout=15)

    # Tick the tree continuously
    try:
        while True:
            behaviour_tree.tick()
            py_trees.timer.sleep(0.5)  # half-
second between ticks
    except KeyboardInterrupt:
        pass

if __name__ == '__main__':
    main()
```

How it Works:

1. **Selector** node: tries WaitForOrder first. If it's still RUNNING, the rest doesn't proceed. Once WaitForOrder returns SUCCESS, the tree moves to the next child (FulfillOrder).
2. **FulfillOrder** is a **Sequence**: GotoPickup, PickupItem, GotoDropoff, DropItem. Each step must succeed before moving on. If any step fails, the sequence can fail or loop, depending on how we handle that logic.

Behavior Tree for Delivery Robot

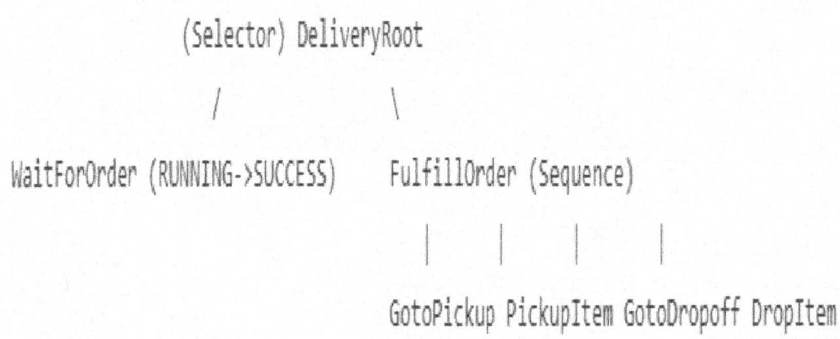

This diagram shows the high-level control flow, with the **Selector** forcing the system to wait for an order before transitioning to fulfillment.

8.3.4 Testing and Extending

- **Simulate** an order: The check_for_new_order() function might read from a ROS2 topic or a mock input.
- **Add Recovery**: Suppose navigation fails. You can handle it by having a **Fallback** or **Selector** node that triggers a "Recovery" subtree if NavigateToLocation fails.
- **Parallel Tasks**: If you want the robot to monitor battery or monitor time constraints while fulfilling the order, you can incorporate a **Parallel** composite.

8.4. Error Recovery and Robustness in Real Environments

Both finite state machines and behavior trees help structure robot logic—but real-world robotics is messy. Sensors can fail, commands might time out, or items might be misplaced. Let's consider strategies to ensure robust operation.

8.4.1 Common Failure Modes

1. **Sensor Disconnects**: The LiDAR or camera feed might drop out.
2. **Actuator Overloads**: Motors might stall or see overcurrent.
3. **Network Issues**: In multi-robot or cloud-based setups, network latency or disconnections can disrupt tasks.
4. **Localization or Navigation Errors**: The robot may be stuck or lose track of its pose.

8.4.2 Handling Errors in an FSM

- **Recovery States**: For each state, define transitions to a "Recover" or "Error" state if an unexpected condition arises.
- **Retry Logic**: If a navigation command fails, you might retry up to N times, then escalate to a higher-level error state.

Example (pseudo-code):

```python
smach.StateMachine.add('NAV',
    NavigateState(),
    transitions={'success': 'NEXT_STATE',
                 'fail': 'RECOVER_NAV'})
...
smach.StateMachine.add('RECOVER_NAV',
    RecoveryState(),
    transitions={'success': 'NAV',
                 'fail': 'ABORT'})
```

8.4.3 Handling Errors in a Behavior Tree

Behavior trees often incorporate **Fallback** or **Selector** nodes. If the primary action fails, the next child node attempts a recovery action.

Example (pseudo-code):

```python
recover_selector =
py_trees.composites.Selector(name="NavOrRecover")
nav_action = NavigateToLocation()
recover_action = RecoveryBehavior()

recover_selector.add_children([nav_action,
recover_action])
```

1. The tree first tries nav_action. If it returns FAILURE, the fallback node attempts recover_action.
2. If recover_action also fails, the composite node might itself fail, which you can handle at a higher level.

8.4.4 Real-World Tips

1. **Watchdogs**: Periodically check if your state machine or behavior tree is stuck in a loop. Implement timeouts or safety overrides.
2. **Logging and Visualization**: Tools like rqt_graph or behavior tree visualizers let you see the current state or node progress.
3. **Graceful Degradation**: If a sensor fails, can the robot continue partially? Or does it need to abort the mission gracefully?
4. **Testing Under Stress**: Simulate partial sensor data drops, artificially insert obstacles, or degrade power levels to see how your logic handles it.

Error Handling with a Fallback Node

```
Fallback (Selector)
   /          \
(Navigate)    (Recover)
  SUCCESS-> done
  FAILURE-> try Recover -> success or fail
```

This simple fallback structure ensures that if navigation fails, the robot tries a recovery strategy.

Conclusion of Chapter 8

Designing **advanced robot behaviors** demands more than just sequences of commands. Structured approaches like **finite state machines** and **behavior trees** bring order to complexity, letting your robot handle branching tasks, real-time reactivity, and robust error recovery. By combining Python tools such as smach or py_trees_ros with careful planning, you can create systems that gracefully handle everything from normal operation to the unexpected realities of hardware failures and dynamic environments.

Key Takeaways

1. **Complexity Management:** FSMs and BTs help you segment large tasks into manageable states or nodes, clarifying logic and easing troubleshooting.
2. **Python Libraries:** smach offers a classical FSM approach, while py_trees_ros embraces hierarchical, reactive patterns. Pick whichever aligns best with your project's style.
3. **Delivery Robot Example:** Illustrates how to chain tasks like waiting for orders, navigating to locations, and picking up items using a behavior tree.
4. **Error Recovery:** Build in fallback behaviors and dedicated recovery states/nodes to handle real-world issues like sensor malfunctions or collisions.
5. **Real-World Resilience:** Rely on watchdogs, thorough testing, and partial redundancy to keep your robot operational even when conditions aren't perfect.

Frequently Asked Questions

1. **Q:** Are behavior trees strictly better than FSMs?
   A: Neither approach is universally better. FSMs are often simpler for linear or limited branching. Behavior trees excel in highly modular, reactive scenarios. Many projects mix or adapt both.
2. **Q:** Can I run a behavior tree inside an FSM, or vice versa?

A: Yes. Hybrid approaches are common—for instance, an FSM's "Action" state might internally run a behavior tree. This can get complicated, so keep an eye on clarity.

3. **Q**: How do I incorporate concurrency (e.g., monitoring a sensor while performing a task) in an FSM or BT?
   A: In FSMs, concurrency might require a "concurrence container" like in smach. In BTs, use a Parallel node or a separate sub-tree that runs in parallel, reacting to changes.
4. **Q**: Are these patterns used beyond mobile robots?
   A: Absolutely. Robot arms, drone swarms, even soft robots can benefit from structured behavior control. Behavior trees are also common in video games, AI agents, and interactive simulations.
5. **Q**: How can I visually debug a behavior tree?
   A: Tools like py_trees_ros include optional viewers or loggers that display the tree and highlight which nodes are running, succeeded, or failed. This is invaluable for complex debugging.

What's Next?

We've established how to structure high-level behaviors. Next steps might include:

- **Advanced AI Integration**: Incorporating machine learning or pattern recognition to dynamically switch between states or behaviors.
- **Multi-Robot Coordination**: Using a shared FSM or distributed behavior tree for fleets of robots.
- **Continuous Improvement:** Logging performance data to refine transitions, reduce failure rates, and evolve your robot's autonomy over time.

In the broader journey of **ROS2 and Python robotics**, combining robust **sensing**, **navigation**, and **behavior design** sets the stage for the truly transformative applications—robots that can adapt, learn, and work side by side with humans in real-world settings.

Chapter 9: Advanced Topics in ROS2 and Python

You've made significant progress, learning how to set up your robotics environment, integrate sensors, manage navigation, and build complex behaviors. Now it's time to dig deeper into **advanced topics** that help push real-world robotics projects to the next level. This chapter covers:

1. **ROS2 Middleware and DDS**: Understanding how ROS2 communicates under the hood and how to leverage its middleware features.
2. **Using Docker and Containers**: Containerization can drastically simplify deployments, making your robot's software portable and consistent.
3. **Remote Monitoring and Control**: Techniques for controlling robots over networks, including cloud integration.
4. **Performance Optimization and Profiling**: Ensuring your Python nodes run efficiently and can handle heavy computational loads.
5. **Hands-On Project**: We'll wrap up with a concrete example of deploying a robot application in a Docker container, showcasing how to apply everything in a reproducible, scalable way.

By the end, you'll be equipped to handle large-scale, distributed, and performance-critical ROS2 projects with Python.

9.1. ROS2 Middleware and DDS (Data Distribution Service)

If you've used ROS2, you already know that nodes communicate via topics, services, and actions. Under the hood, ROS2 uses something called **DDS (Data Distribution Service)** as its middleware—essentially the "plumbing" that handles discovery, serialization, and transport of messages. Understanding the basics of DDS can help you optimize or troubleshoot distributed systems.

9.1.1 What is DDS?

DDS is a standardized pub-sub communication protocol designed for distributed real-time systems. It automatically handles:

1. **Discovery**: How nodes find each other on the network without manual configuration.
2. **QoS (Quality of Service) Settings**: Letting you specify reliability, durability, and deadlines for different data streams.
3. **Data-Centric Model**: DDS focuses on how data is shared, not just point-to-point communications.

ROS2 is built on top of **DDS** using an abstraction layer called the **ROS Middleware Interface** (RMW). Different DDS vendors (e.g., **Fast-DDS**, **CycloneDDS**, **RTI Connext**) can be plugged in to suit your needs—some are open-source, others commercial.

9.1.2 Why DDS Matters

1. **Scalability**: DDS can handle dozens or hundreds of nodes across multiple machines, a boon for large robotics systems (like factory floors).
2. **Real-Time Features**: Some vendors offer real-time guarantees if you configure QoS parameters appropriately.
3. **Flexibility**: You can tune reliability, bandwidth usage, and discovery to fit your environment—LAN, WAN, or ad-hoc networks.

9.1.3 ROS2 QoS Settings

Quality of Service (QoS) policies in ROS2 let you adjust how data is sent and received:

- **Reliability**: Best Effort vs. Reliable. Best Effort might drop messages if the network is congested, while Reliable ensures each message arrives (but at a potential performance cost).
- **Durability**: Volatile vs. Transient Local. Transient means new subscribers can receive older messages queued by the publisher.

- **Deadline:** Tells the system how often messages must arrive. Missing a deadline can trigger callbacks or reconfiguration.

Example (Python snippet configuring QoS):

```
python


import rclpy
from rclpy.node import Node
from std_msgs.msg import String
from rclpy.qos import QoSProfile,
ReliabilityPolicy

class QoSNode(Node):
    def __init__(self):
        super().__init__('qos_node')
        qos_profile = QoSProfile(
            depth=10,

reliability=ReliabilityPolicy.RELIABLE
        )
        self.publisher_ =
self.create_publisher(String, 'my_topic',
qos_profile)
        # ...
```

ROS2 over DDS

```
[ROS2 Node A] ----> RMW layer ----> DDS Vendor (e.g. Cyclone)
[ROS2 Node B] ----> RMW layer ----> DDS Vendor (e.g. Fast-DDS)
[ROS2 Node C] ----> RMW layer ----> DDS Vendor (e.g. RTI Connext)

      |---------- Data Exchange via Network ---------|
```

Nodes use RMW to talk to a DDS vendor, which handles data distribution across the network.

9.2. Using Docker and Containers for Robotics Deployments

Setting up a ROS2 project can be complex: multiple packages, specific library versions, drivers, and environment variables. **Docker** simplifies this by wrapping everything in a container, ensuring consistent deployments across different machines.

9.2.1 Why Containers?

1. **Portability**: A Docker image runs the same on your local PC, on a cloud VM, or on an SBC like a Jetson (with some platform-specific considerations).
2. **Isolation**: Container boundaries reduce conflicts between dependencies.

3. **Reproducibility:** If it works in your Docker container, it should work anywhere else that runs the same container.

9.2.2 Basic Docker Workflow

1. **Dockerfile:** A text file specifying how to build your image—what base OS to use, which packages to install, and how to set up ROS2.
2. **docker build:** Creates an image from the Dockerfile.
3. **docker run:** Starts a container from that image.
4. **docker-compose** (optional): Orchestrates multi-container setups, handy if you want separate containers for database, robot software, etc.

9.2.3 Common Docker Practices in Robotics

- **Multi-Stage Builds:** You might compile your ROS2 workspace in one stage, then copy the resulting binaries into a lightweight runtime image.
- **Volumes:** Mount hardware devices (e.g., /dev/ttyUSB0) or persistent data so that logs or calibration files persist outside the container.
- **Networking:** Docker networking can be tricky, especially if you want DDS discovery across multiple machines. You might need to configure host networking or specify your DDS participant settings.

Example Dockerfile (simplified):

```dockerfile
FROM ros:humble-ros-core  # Official ROS2 base image

# Install dependencies
RUN apt-get update && apt-get install -y \
    python3-colcon-common-extensions \
    build-essential

# Create workspace
WORKDIR /robot_ws
COPY src/ ./src

# Build
RUN . /opt/ros/humble/setup.sh && colcon build

# Source entrypoint
ENTRYPOINT ["/bin/bash", "-c", "source /opt/ros/humble/setup.sh && source install/setup.sh && bash"]
```

9.3. Remote Monitoring and Control (ROS2 over networks, cloud integration)

Modern robotics often extends beyond a single machine or local network. You might want to **teleoperate** a robot from across the country or collect sensor data in the cloud for advanced analytics.

9.3.1 ROS2 Over WAN

By default, DDS-based discovery is oriented toward LANs. For wide-area networks or NAT-traversed connections, you'll need some additional configuration:

1. **VPN or SSH Tunneling**: Simplify the network by creating a VPN so all machines appear on the same LAN.
2. **DDS Router or Gateway**: Some DDS vendors provide specialized routers that forward traffic from one domain to another.
3. **Static Configuration**: If auto-discovery fails, you can manually specify participant addresses or use a bridging approach.

9.3.2 Cloud Integration

Robots increasingly leverage cloud services for:

- **Data Storage**: Large sensor datasets, logs, or images.

- **Computation:** Offload heavy tasks like machine learning inference or SLAM to a powerful cloud instance.
- **Fleet Management:** A web dashboard for multiple robots, running in a centralized cloud environment.

Techniques:

- **ROS2 Bridge to MQTT or WebSockets:** Some solutions let you forward ROS2 topics to a cloud messaging system for real-time dashboards or analytics.
- **Edge Computing:** Keep latency-sensitive tasks (like obstacle avoidance) on the robot, but send high-level data to the cloud for analysis or training.

Example: A warehouse robot might locally run Nav2 for real-time navigation, but it sends aggregated sensor data to AWS or Azure IoT for inventory analytics or big-picture route optimization.

Hybrid Cloud-Robot Setup

```
Robot SBC (ROS2) -- DDS-based local messaging
       ^                  |
       | (Publish/Subscribe)
       v                  |
Onboard Microcontrollers
                                 Internet
                                     |
                  +----------------------+
                  |  Cloud Instance      |
                  |  Analytics, ML, etc|
                  +----------------------+
```

The robot handles immediate control, while the cloud does heavier data crunching or coordination.

9.4. Performance Optimization and Profiling Python Nodes

Python is beloved for its readability but can be a bottleneck if you're running computationally heavy tasks. In robotics, sensor data can arrive at high frequency, so it's crucial to ensure your nodes aren't bogging down the system.

9.4.1 Profiling Basics

1. **time**: Simple approach to measure how long a script takes overall. Not fine-grained, but easy to start with.
2. **cProfile**: A built-in Python profiler that shows you function call times.
3. **SnakeViz** or **RunSnakeRun**: Tools that visualize cProfile output, highlighting where your code spends the most time.

Example:

```bash

python -m cProfile -o profile_data.out
my_python_node.py
snakeviz profile_data.out
```

You can then see a web-based breakdown of function calls and time spent.

9.4.2 Common Bottlenecks

- **Excessive Loops in Python**: E.g., looping over large arrays without using NumPy's vectorized operations.
- **String Manipulations**: Unnecessary concatenations or frequent logging can add overhead.
- **Data Conversions**: Repeatedly converting message formats or images if not careful.

- **Synchronous I/O**: Blocking operations while waiting for sensor data or network calls.

9.4.3 Solutions

1. **Leverage NumPy**: Move math-heavy tasks to NumPy, which uses optimized C libraries under the hood.
2. **Cython or C++ Extensions**: If a certain function is a major bottleneck, port it to a C++ extension.
3. **Asynchronous Patterns**: Use async calls or concurrency (though Python's GIL can limit true parallelism).
4. **ROS2 Nodes in C++**: If performance is critical (like high-rate sensor processing), consider rewriting time-critical parts in C++, leaving high-level logic in Python.

9.4.4 Real-Time or Near Real-Time Considerations

For truly real-time constraints (like controlling a quadcopter's flight control loops at 1kHz), Python might be too slow or unpredictable. In these cases, you'd typically:

- Place critical loops on a **microcontroller** or in a **C++** node with real-time OS support.
- Let Python handle higher-level coordination or UI tasks.

9.5. Hands-On Project: Deploying a Robot Application in a Docker Container

Let's tie these advanced concepts together with a step-by-step project. We'll **build**, **containerize**, and **run** a simple ROS2 robot application in Docker—one that can be monitored remotely and scaled to different devices.

9.5.1 Project Overview

1. **Simple Application:** A Python node that publishes sensor data (simulated) and subscribes to a command topic, controlling a mock motor.
2. **Dockerfile**: We'll create an image that includes ROS2 (Humble, for example) and our package.
3. **Container Execution**: We'll run the container on a local machine or SBC, ensuring it can access hardware if needed (e.g., a USB sensor).
4. **Remote Access**: We'll demonstrate how to connect to the container from another machine, echoing topics or sending commands.

9.5.2 Setting Up the Project

Folder Structure:

markdown

```
docker_robot_app/
├── Dockerfile
├── src
│   ├── robot_sensor_pub
│   │   ├── __init__.py
│   │   └── sensor_node.py
│   └── robot_motor_sub
│       ├── __init__.py
│       └── motor_node.py
├── setup.py
├── package.xml
└── README.md
```

sensor_node.py (mock sensor publisher):

```python
python

import rclpy
from rclpy.node import Node
from std_msgs.msg import Float32
import random
import time

class SensorNode(Node):
    def __init__(self):
        super().__init__('sensor_node')
        self.publisher_ =
self.create_publisher(Float32, 'sensor_data', 10)
```

```
        self.timer = self.create_timer(1.0,
self.publish_data)

    def publish_data(self):
        msg = Float32()
        msg.data = random.uniform(0, 100)  # mock
sensor
        self.publisher_.publish(msg)
        self.get_logger().info(f"Publishing
sensor data: {msg.data}")

def main(args=None):
    rclpy.init(args=args)
    node = SensorNode()
    rclpy.spin(node)
    node.destroy_node()
    rclpy.shutdown()

if __name__ == '__main__':
    main()
```

motor_node.py (mock motor subscriber):

```
python

import rclpy
from rclpy.node import Node
from geometry_msgs.msg import Twist

class MotorNode(Node):
```

```
    def __init__(self):
        super().__init__('motor_node')
        self.subscription =
self.create_subscription(
            Twist,
            'cmd_vel',
            self.cmd_callback,
            10)

    def cmd_callback(self, msg):
        # Just log the commands for now
        linear_x = msg.linear.x
        angular_z = msg.angular.z
        self.get_logger().info(f"Received
cmd_vel: linear={linear_x}, angular={angular_z}")

def main(args=None):
    rclpy.init(args=args)
    node = MotorNode()
    rclpy.spin(node)
    node.destroy_node()
    rclpy.shutdown()

if __name__ == '__main__':
    main()
```

9.5.3 Dockerfile

```
dockerfile
```

```
# Use an official ROS2 base
FROM ros:humble-ros-core

# Install necessary packages for colcon build
RUN apt-get update && apt-get install -y \
    python3-colcon-common-extensions

# Create a workspace
WORKDIR /robot_ws

# Copy package files
COPY ./src ./src
COPY package.xml .
COPY setup.py .

# Build the ROS2 workspace
RUN . /opt/ros/humble/setup.sh && colcon build

# Source the workspace upon container start
COPY entrypoint.sh /entrypoint.sh
RUN chmod +x /entrypoint.sh
ENTRYPOINT ["/entrypoint.sh"]
CMD ["bash"]
```

entrypoint.sh:

```
bash

#!/bin/bash
```

```
source /opt/ros/humble/setup.bash
cd /robot_ws
source install/setup.bash
exec "$@"
```

9.5.4 Building and Running the Container

1. **Build:**

```bash
docker build -t robot_app:v1 .
```

Run *(foreground terminal):*

```bash
docker run -it --rm robot_app:v1
```

Inside the container, you can now launch your nodes:

```bash
ros2 run robot_sensor_pub sensor_node
# In another terminal (docker exec -it
<container_id> bash):
ros2 run robot_motor_sub motor_node
```

2. **Test** by publishing commands from your host:

```bash
ros2 topic pub /cmd_vel geometry_msgs/msg/Twist
"{linear: {x: 1.0}, angular: {z: 0.5}}"
```

You should see the motor_node in the container log the received cmd_vel messages.

9.5.5 Remote Access Considerations

- **Network Bridge**: By default, Docker uses a NATed network. For ROS2 discovery to work, you may need --net=host on Linux or more advanced bridging.
- **VPN**: If controlling from outside your local network, set up a VPN or SSH tunnel into the host machine.

Dockerized ROS2 Application

```
+-----------------------+
| Docker Container      |  (sensor_node, motor_node)
|   /robot_ws           |
|   source install/setup |
+---------+-------------+
          |
 Host OS  | -> /dev/tty... or net=host
          |
Outside Clients (remote PC)  -> publish /cmd_vel, subscribe /sensor_data
```

Conclusion of Chapter 9

In this chapter, we ventured into **advanced** ROS2 and Python topics that empower robotics projects at scale:

1. **ROS2 Middleware and DDS**: You learned the fundamental building blocks of ROS2 networking, including QoS settings for reliability, speed, and other constraints.
2. **Docker:** A powerful tool to containerize your entire ROS2 environment, ensuring reproducible deployments across devices or operating systems.
3. **Remote Monitoring and Control:** Best practices for running ROS2 nodes across LAN/WAN, interfacing with cloud services, and bridging big data or advanced analytics.
4. **Performance Optimization**: Profiling Python nodes, identifying bottlenecks, and employing strategies for faster, more efficient code.
5. **Hands-On Deployment:** A concrete walkthrough of building, running, and testing a Dockerized ROS2 application.

Key Takeaways

- **DDS Underpins ROS2**: Understanding DDS helps you optimize and debug distributed robotics networks.
- **Containers Simplify Deployments**: Docker containers let you package all dependencies, making your robot software portable and consistent.

- **Remote Access:** With the right network configurations (VPN, tunnels, or DDS bridging), you can manage robots from virtually anywhere.
- **Profile and Optimize:** Python is versatile but can be slow if used naively. Profiling tools reveal where to optimize or offload tasks to C++ or hardware accelerators.
- **Scalable Workflows:** The Docker-based approach ensures that, as your project grows, you can spin up identical environments for each robot or developer.

Frequently Asked Questions

1. **Q:** Is DDS mandatory for all ROS2 setups?
   A: Yes, ROS2 relies on DDS (though multiple vendor implementations exist). You can't replace DDS with a completely different protocol without significant changes to the ROS2 core.
2. **Q:** Can I run GUI tools (like RViz) inside a Docker container?
   A: Yes, but you'll need to forward X11 or use a VNC server in the container. Alternatively, run RViz on the host and connect to containerized nodes.
3. **Q:** How do I handle GPU-accelerated tasks in Docker for robotics?
   A: Use **nvidia-docker** or similar solutions if you need CUDA or GPU resources. Just ensure your Docker container has access to the GPU drivers on the host.

4. **Q**: My WAN is unreliable. How do I ensure my remote commands still get through?
   A: You might choose **Reliable** QoS, but that alone won't solve all WAN issues. Often, a bridging or store-and-forward approach is best. Or maintain a stable VPN connection with fallback logic.

5. **Q**: When should I use Python vs. C++ for performance-critical nodes?
   A: If you're doing heavy sensor processing at high rates (e.g., 100+ Hz LiDAR scans), C++ might be necessary. For less time-critical logic, or for prototyping, Python is quick and easier to iterate with.

What's Next?

Equipped with these advanced techniques, you're ready to tackle **large-scale**, **networked**, and **performance-critical** robotic applications. In future chapters or personal explorations, consider:

- **Multi-Robot Coordination**: Containerizing each robot's stack and orchestrating them with Docker Compose or Kubernetes.
- **Edge-Cloud Hybrids**: Offloading compute-intensive tasks to a cloud GPU while keeping local real-time control.
- **AI/ML Integration**: Dockerizing deep learning frameworks (e.g., PyTorch) to run in tandem with

your ROS2 nodes for advanced perception or decision-making.

With robust deployments, remote management, and optimized performance, your ROS2-based robots can be deployed in factories, hospitals, or fields—and keep running reliably under challenging conditions.

Chapter 10: Practical Applications and Case Studies

Robotics has rapidly evolved from theoretical research labs to real-world applications spanning factories, healthcare facilities, city streets, and even distant planets. If you've followed the journey so far—learning about sensors, navigation, planning, and advanced ROS2 concepts—you're now prepared to see how these skills can **transform entire industries** and enable feats once thought impossible. In this chapter, we'll take a tour of practical robotics applications, showcasing how the concepts we've covered find life in **manufacturing**, **healthcare**, **logistics**, and **space exploration**. We'll also highlight a **real-world multi-robot coordination** project—illustrating how everything ties together for a cause as critical as **disaster response**.

By the end, you'll gain **inspiration** for how to apply your newfound robotics skills in various domains—and see how different technologies converge to create cutting-edge robotic solutions.

10.1. Manufacturing and Warehouse Robotics (Autonomous Mobile Robots, Conveyors)

When you imagine a high-tech **production line** or **vast warehouse**, you likely picture robots swiftly sorting packages, assembling parts, and moving goods around. Manufacturing and warehouse environments are among the largest adopters of robotics—why? Because robots **excel** at tasks that require precision, speed, and repetitive motion.

10.1.1 Autonomous Mobile Robots (AMRs)

Autonomous Mobile Robots are a step beyond traditional Automated Guided Vehicles (AGVs). While AGVs often follow fixed tracks or magnetic strips, AMRs navigate **dynamically** using sensors like LiDAR or cameras, a built-in navigation stack, and **path planning** algorithms. In large e-commerce or fulfillment centers, these robots:

1. **Avoid Collisions**: Using onboard sensors (e.g., LiDAR, depth cameras) to detect and circumvent humans, shelves, or other robots.
2. **Localize and Map**: Often employing SLAM or local navigation on a pre-mapped facility.
3. **Coordinate**: They share location data or receive dispatch commands from a central system that optimizes routes based on real-time load.

Key Benefits:

- **Flexibility:** You can easily reconfigure a warehouse layout without reprogramming robots.
- **Scalability:** Add more AMRs as demand grows, each plugging into the same navigation and dispatch software.
- **Reduced Operational Costs:** Minimizing manual labor for repetitive transport tasks.

AMR in a Warehouse

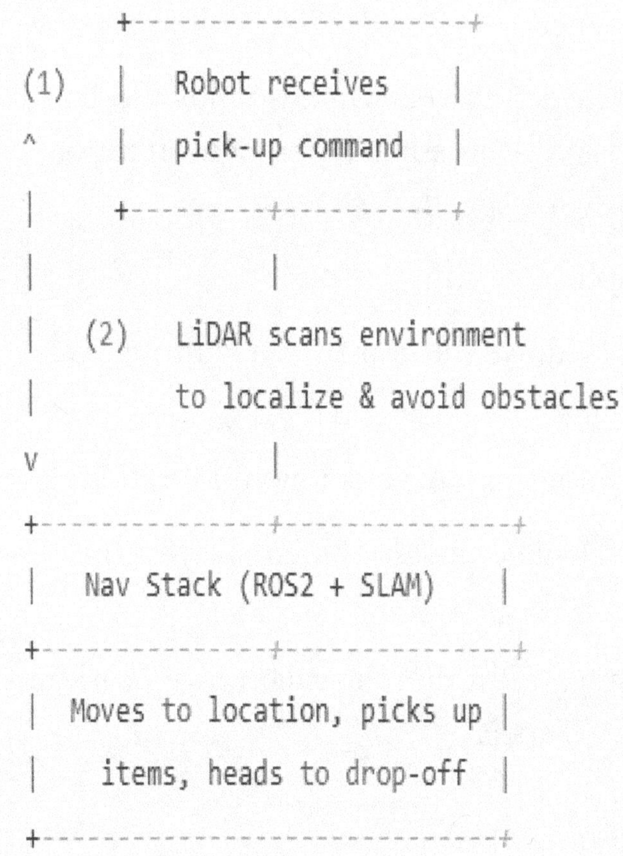
(1)
Robot receives
pick-up command
(2)
LiDAR scans environment
to localize & avoid obstacles
Nav Stack (ROS2 + SLAM)
Moves to location, picks up
items, heads to drop-off

10.1.2 Conveyor Systems with Robot Integration

In many factories, **conveyor belts** serve as arteries, moving products from one station to the next. Robots supplement these conveyors by **picking** or **placing** items onto them. For instance:

- **Robotic Arms** at the end of a conveyor to perform quality inspection or assembly tasks.
- **Vision Systems** that detect orientation, letting the robot pick up each item precisely, even if it's randomly oriented.
- **ROS2** (with relevant drivers) orchestrating the arm's movement, vision processing, and synchronization with the conveyor's speed.

Step-by-Step Example

1. **Camera** hovers above the conveyor, capturing real-time images.
2. **OpenCV** identifies part orientation and position.
3. **ROS2** node calculates inverse kinematics for the robotic arm.
4. **Arm** picks the part if within the valid range or triggers an error if out of spec.

Benefits:

- Consistency of product handling, reducing defects or accidents.
- Easy reprogramming for new product lines—just update the detection or pick-and-place logic.

10.1.3 Challenges

1. **Workplace Safety:** Humans often still share space with robots or conveyors. Ensuring safe collaboration is key.
2. **Frequent Layout Changes:** A dynamic warehouse might require robust localization and adaptive software.
3. **Integration Complexity:** Mixing different vendors' robots, conveyors, and software can lead to compatibility issues—where robust, open communication standards like ROS2 help.

10.2. Healthcare Robotics (Patient Assistance, Telepresence)

Robots in healthcare do more than futuristic surgeries—they support patient care, rehabilitation, and even remote consultations. The rising aging population and global healthcare staff shortages amplify the need for such helpers.

10.2.1 Patient Assistance Robots

Picture a **patient-assistance robot** in a rehabilitation center. It can:

1. **Lift and Transfer Patients** from bed to wheelchair using sensors to gauge weight distribution and prevent injury.
2. **Aid in Exercise**: Exoskeletons help patients walk, guided by IMUs and feedback loops for stable motion.
3. **Deliver Medication**: Mobile robots navigate hospital corridors, bringing meds to patient rooms on schedule.

Core Tech:

- **Precise Force/Torque Sensors**: Prevent harming the patient.
- **Advanced Controls**: Real-time feedback controlling exoskeleton motors or robotic arms.
- **User-Friendly Interfaces**: Touchscreen or voice activation for patients who can't operate complex devices.

10.2.2 Telepresence and Remote Care

Telepresence robots let doctors or family members interact with patients remotely:

- **Video and Audio Feeds**: High-resolution cameras, mic, and speakers.
- **Mobility**: The robot can roam hospital floors or patient rooms, often using a differential drive with obstacle avoidance.
- **ROS2**: Manages camera streams, two-way audio, and remote commands, possibly via a secure VPN or cloud-based bridging.

Benefits:

- **Reduced Infection Risk**: Minimizing physical contact in isolation wards (e.g., during pandemics).
- **Extended Access**: A specialist in another city or country can evaluate patients more seamlessly.

10.2.3 Challenges

- **Regulatory Hurdles**: Medical robots often require compliance with strict safety and data-privacy standards (e.g., HIPAA in the US).
- **Human Acceptance**: Many patients are initially uncomfortable with robots. Good user experience design is paramount.
- **Cost**: Some advanced robotic systems remain expensive, limiting widespread adoption.

A Telepresence Robot in a Hospital

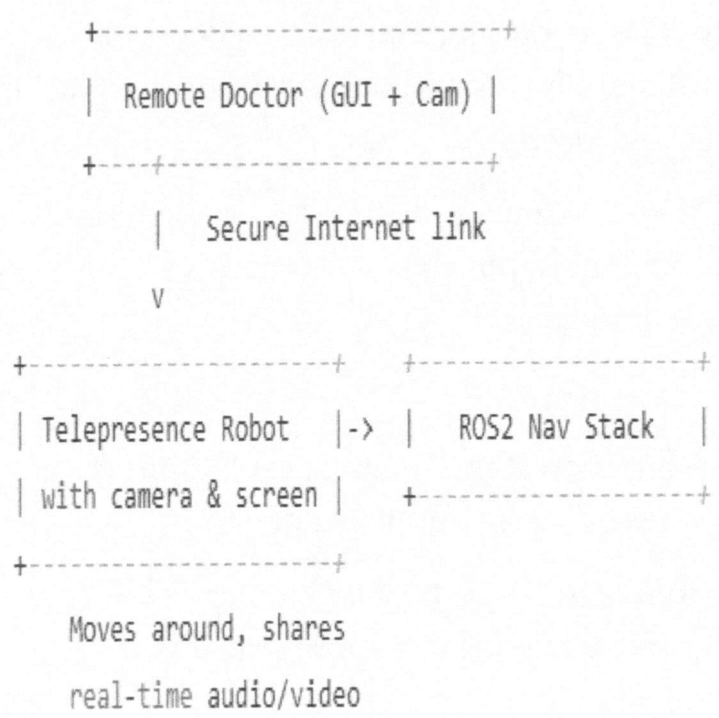

10.3. Logistics and Delivery (Last-Mile Delivery Robots)

Last-mile delivery is among the trickiest and most expensive parts of the supply chain—driving many companies to explore autonomous **delivery robots** or drones. Imagine a small six-wheeled robot rolling down sidewalks or a flying drone dropping off packages at your doorstep.

10.3.1 Sidewalk Delivery Robots

These robots typically carry groceries or small parcels, traveling at safe speeds on sidewalks:

1. **Sensors:** Cameras, LiDAR, ultrasonic sensors to detect pedestrians, curbs, or obstacles.
2. **Remote Supervision:** If they encounter a tricky situation, a human operator might take over or provide guidance.
3. **Navigation:** Combines a local path planner with high-level GPS waypoints. They often rely on object detection to stop for crossing pedestrians or traffic lights.

Benefits:

- **Reduced Traffic Congestion:** No large vans needed for small deliveries.
- **24/7 Operation:** They can run day or night, as long as sidewalks are accessible.
- **Cost Savings:** Over time, a fleet of robots might be cheaper than repeated human-driven trips.

10.3.2 Aerial Drones for Delivery

Drones bring their own challenges:

1. **Flight Regulations:** Must comply with local aviation authorities.

2. **Payload Limits:** Usually small unless you have large, specialized drones.
3. **Obstacle Avoidance:** Requires advanced sensors to avoid power lines, buildings, or birds.

ROS2 can orchestrate flight control, sensor fusion (e.g., GPS + IMU + LiDAR), and teleoperation. With the right hardware, drones can deliver medicine to remote areas or help paramedics in emergency situations.

10.3.3 Challenges

- **Autonomy vs. Teleoperation:** Fully autonomous navigation in unpredictable urban environments remains complex.
- **Security:** Delivery robots can be vandalized or stolen.
- **Infrastructure:** Many cities lack clear rules for sidewalk robots or drone flights.

DLast-Mile Delivery Robot Workflow

```
Customer places order -> Cloud dispatch system
          | (assigns route, time)
          v
  Delivery Robot (sidewalk AMR)
  +-----------------------------+
  | Cameras, LiDAR, GPS, IMU    |
  | ROS2 Nav + Behavior Tree    |
  +-------------+---------------+
                |
          Arrives at door,
       sends notification or
      digital handshake for
      item handover
```

10.4. Space Exploration: Applying Advanced Robotic Systems Concepts

Robotics truly shines **beyond Earth**—where harsh conditions, extreme temperatures, and communication delays make human presence challenging. **Rovers** on Mars or the Moon, robotic arms on the International Space Station, or satellites with autonomous docking capabilities all rely on advanced robotics principles.

10.4.1 Planetary Rovers

- **NASA's Mars Rovers** (Spirit, Opportunity, Curiosity, Perseverance) exemplify robust design. They handle:
    1. **Harsh Environment:** Dust storms, extreme temperature swings.
    2. **Autonomous Driving:** Delays in communication mean rovers must decide how to traverse rocky terrain.
    3. **Energy Constraints:** They often run on solar or nuclear power, prioritizing tasks carefully.
- **SLAM**: Some rovers use visual odometry and mapping to navigate boulder-filled landscapes.
- **Localization:** GPS is unavailable off Earth, so rovers rely on inertial sensors, star trackers, or ground-based triangulation from Earth.

10.4.2 Space Station Robotics

- **Robotic Arms** like **Canadarm** and **Dextre** handle cargo transfers or repair tasks.
- **Internal Astrobee Robots**: Autonomous free-flying robots inside the ISS that help with inventory, camera tasks, and minor chores. They use structured light or LiDAR-based navigation, integrated with a NASA variant of ROS.

Key Concepts:

- **Fault Tolerance:** If a sensor or motor fails, the mission can't rely on quick replacement. Systems must handle partial failures gracefully.
- **Radiation-Hardened Hardware:** Standard microcontrollers or LiDAR might degrade under high radiation; specialized components or shielding is required.
- **Delayed Communication:** Round-trip signals to Mars can be 20 minutes or more, necessitating high autonomy.

10.4.3 Future Directions

- **Moon Bases** with robotic construction teams building habitats from regolith.
- **Asteroid Mining:** Autonomous systems to locate and extract resources with minimal human intervention.
- **Interplanetary Supply Lines:** Coordinating multiple robots (landers, rovers, orbiters) for exploration and resource gathering.

10.5. Real-World Project Example: Multi-Robot Coordination for Disaster Response

Natural disasters—earthquakes, floods, wildfires—often leave areas too hazardous for human first responders. Enter **multi-robot coordination:** a fleet of robots that can **search, map,** and **deliver supplies** swiftly. Let's explore a hypothetical but **realistic** project tying together many ROS2 concepts.

10.5.1 Project Scenario

1. **Objective:** Deploy a team of ground robots to search for survivors and a swarm of aerial drones to map a large disaster zone.
2. **Hardware:**
    - **Ground Robots:** Differential-drive or Ackermann platforms with LiDAR and thermal cameras.
    - **Aerial Drones:** Quadcopters with GPS, cameras, and lightweight LiDAR.
3. **Software:**
    - **ROS2** for communication across all robots.
    - A **central mission control** node for operator oversight.

- Dockerized containers for consistent deployment across heterogeneous robots.
- **Custom Behavior Trees** or state machines controlling search patterns, obstacle avoidance, and data gathering.

10.5.2 Step-by-Step Approach

Let's break down how you might set up such a system.

1. Planning & Mapping

- **Preliminary Satellite Data**: Obtain local topography.
- **Nav2** on Each Robot**: Each ground robot uses local navigation with costmaps updated by LiDAR and ultrasonic sensors.
- **Collaborative SLAM**: As they explore, their sensor data merges into a global map stored on a local server or in the cloud.

2. Role Assignment and Dispatch

- **Central Control**: Assigns tasks like "Sector A scanning" to Drone 1, "Rubble clearing" to Ground Robot 2, etc.
- **Behavior Tree**: Each robot's high-level logic determines whether it's searching, returning for recharge, or assisting another unit.

3. Communication

- **Mesh Network:** In a disaster zone, infrastructure might be down, so robots create an ad-hoc network.
- **DDS Over Wi-Fi:** Some robots connect directly, others via bridging nodes for extended range.
- **Cloud Relay** (if available): If a connection to the internet remains, global stakeholders can monitor progress.

4. **Data Collection**

- **Thermal Camera Feeds:** Identify hotspots or survivors.
- **High-Resolution Photogrammetry** from drones, building a 3D model.
- **ROS2 Bag Recording:** Each robot logs data for post-mission analysis or real-time crisis management.

5. **Multi-Robot Coordination**

- **Swarm Intelligence:** Possibly employing algorithms that reduce overlap in scanning or systematically cover areas.
- **Real-Time Obstacle Alerts:** If Drone 2 spots a collapsed building, ground robots get a re-routing or hazard update.
- **Resource Sharing:** If Robot A's battery runs low, Robot B can handle tasks in that sector or guide Robot A back to a charging point.

6. Handling Failure

- **Redundancy:** If a drone fails, others can fill the gap.
- **Self-Diagnosis:** Robots detect sensor malfunctions (like a LiDAR returning nonsense data), triggering fallback behaviors.
- **Human Intervention:** A teleoperator might take remote control of a partially functioning robot or override tasks for urgent missions.

10.5.3 Visualizing the Operation

Each robot runs its own local ROS2 navigation, while a central node coordinates tasks, merges map data, and handles operator inputs. The entire architecture can be containerized in Docker images for easy deployment on any hardware.

10.5.4 Practical Outcomes

- **Saving Lives:** Faster, safer exploration of hazardous areas to find survivors or deliver critical supplies.
- **Scalability:** Add or remove robots as needed, each one connecting to the mesh network.
- **Continuous Improvement:** Data logs feed machine learning models that refine search patterns or obstacle avoidance for the next disaster scenario.

Conclusion of Chapter 10

From the controlled environment of a **manufacturing floor** to the unpredictable terrain of **Mars**, robots find countless real-world applications. **Warehouses**, **healthcare facilities**, and **last-mile delivery** services all leverage robotics to boost efficiency, enhance safety, and serve people in ways previously unimaginable. Advanced robotics also enables **multi-robot cooperation** for high-stakes missions like disaster response, showcasing the power of distributed AI, robust sensing, and autonomy.

Key Takeaways

1. **Cross-Industry Impact**: Robots are transforming nearly every sector, from e-commerce to healthcare.
2. **Common Threads**: Regardless of domain, you'll find **sensing**, **navigation**, **behavior control**, and **cloud connectivity**.
3. **Scalability**: As technology matures, smaller companies and nonprofits can also deploy robots, not just huge corporations or agencies.
4. **Human-Centric Approach**: Real-world success demands user acceptance, safety, and regulatory compliance—beyond just technical feats.
5. **Complex Coordination**: Multi-robot systems exemplify the synergy of networking, advanced control, and collective intelligence.

Frequently Asked Questions

1. **Q**: Which domain is growing fastest for robotics?
   A: E-commerce and warehousing see massive growth, but healthcare and agriculture are also expanding rapidly.
2. **Q**: Are these domains all using ROS2?
   A: Many do, especially in prototyping and advanced research. However, some large players use proprietary or hybrid systems with ROS2 bridging.
3. **Q**: How does one break into specialized fields like space robotics?
   A: Typically, through specialized programs or research collaborations (NASA, ESA, or private aerospace companies). Building a strong foundation in autonomy, mechatronics, and reliability is essential.
4. **Q**: Are there real code examples for multi-robot disaster response?
   A: While some open-source projects exist (e.g., "RobotX Challenge," "DARPA SubT"), many advanced solutions remain proprietary or in research labs. Still, you can adapt open-source multi-robot frameworks in ROS2 for your use case.
5. **Q**: Is it feasible for small businesses or startups to adopt robotics in these domains?
   A: Absolutely. Lower-cost hardware, open-source software (like ROS2), and rapid development tools

(Python, Docker) make robotics more accessible than ever.

What's Next?

With these case studies, you've seen **ROS2 and Python** applied to a diverse range of scenarios. Consider your own passions or business needs. Could you adapt an autonomous mobile robot to a new environment? Or build a telepresence solution for remote medical consultation? The possibilities are broad. Up next, you'll find **how to build a complete robot from scratch** or expand on advanced topics like multi-robot control or AI integration. Whichever path you choose, you now have a wealth of **inspiration** and **practical direction** to guide your next steps in the real world of robotics.

Chapter 11: Building a Complete Robot from Scratch

Throughout this book, we've explored ROS2 fundamentals, Python essentials, navigation, perception, and more. Now it's time to **put it all together** and build an actual robot from scratch—a process that blends **mechanical design**, **electronics**, **software integration**, and **iterative testing**. In this chapter, we'll walk through conceptualizing your robot's goals and requirements, outline critical mechanical design considerations, discuss integrating sensors and behaviors, then dive into a **hands-on project** for constructing a mobile robot with ROS2 and Python. We'll close by discussing how to test, refine, and learn from mistakes so that you can continue evolving your design.

By the end, you'll have the blueprint—and confidence—to tackle a **full-scale robotics project** of your own, bringing together mechanical components, electronics, ROS2-based software, and Python scripts.

11.1. Conceptualizing Your Robot: Goals, Requirements, and Constraints

Every successful robotics build starts with a **clear vision.** Whether you're creating a line-following robot for a competition, a warehouse bot for material handling, or a household helper, defining the **purpose** and **constraints** upfront will save countless hours and headaches down the road.

11.1.1 Establishing Goals

1. **Primary Function:** What do you want the robot to do? Examples:
    - Navigate autonomously in an indoor environment.
    - Carry objects from one location to another.
    - Serve as a platform for teaching robotics in a classroom.
2. **Environment:** Is your robot operating on smooth floors, outdoors, or in a cluttered environment?
3. **Interaction:** Will your robot interact with humans? If so, how? Voice commands, a touchscreen, or something else?

These questions shape your design decisions—like sensor selection, mechanical drive type, and interface preferences.

11.1.2 Functional Requirements

- **Mobility**: Do you need differential drive, Ackermann steering, tracked locomotion, or a walking mechanism?
- **Payload Capacity**: How heavy are the items you might transport?
- **Runtime**: Battery life, or does the robot need to be powered from the grid?
- **Communication**: Will it rely on Wi-Fi, Ethernet, or a 4G/5G link?

11.1.3 Constraints

1. **Budget**: High-end sensors (e.g., 3D LiDAR, industrial arms) can be pricey. If you're a hobbyist, you might prioritize lower-cost alternatives.
2. **Size and Weight**: If your environment has narrow doorways or weight restrictions, design accordingly.
3. **Timeframe**: A project for a semester-long course differs from a multi-year R&D project at a startup.
4. **Safety and Regulations**: If you operate near people, consider collision avoidance, safety standards, or country-specific rules (especially for drones or large robots).

***Analogy**: Building a robot is like constructing a house: you need a blueprint (goals/requirements), materials that fit the* *environment, and a plan to ensure everything (foundation, walls, plumbing, wiring) works together. The more specific your blueprint, the fewer last-minute changes you'll face.*

11.2. Mechanical Design Considerations (Chassis, Wheels, Grippers)

Once you've nailed down the robot's purpose and environment, it's time to design the **mechanical framework**—the chassis, wheels, possible arms or grippers, and how each piece supports your goals.

11.2.1 Chassis Types

1. **Four-Wheeled Rectangular Base:** Common and stable, often used for indoor rovers or small-scale warehouse bots.
2. **Three-Wheeled:** Typically two powered wheels plus a caster, simplifying differential drive.
3. **Tracked:** Great for rough terrain, though it can complicate turning precision and add mechanical complexity.
4. **Omnidirectional:** Mecanum or omnidirectional wheels enable sideways movement, beneficial in tight indoor spaces but more complex to control.

Step-by-Step: Choosing a Chassis

1. **List Requirements**: Payload capacity, turning radius, environment specifics (flat floor vs. uneven ground).
2. **Assess Materials**: 3D-printed plastic, aluminum, steel, wood, or acrylic. Consider weight vs. durability vs. cost.
3. **Draft or Model**: Use CAD tools (Fusion 360, SolidWorks, or FreeCAD) to visualize the layout.
4. **Prototype**: Build a quick mock-up using cardboard or laser-cut plastic to check dimensions before final assembly.

11.2.2 Wheels and Drive Systems

Drive System:

- **Differential Drive**: Two wheels independently driven; simplest to implement in ROS2 with a standard control plugin.
- **Ackermann Steering**: Car-like steering, good for higher speeds or outdoor navigation.
- **Holonomic Drive**: Mecanum or omni-wheels, enabling lateral movement.

Wheel Selection:

- **Diameter**: Larger wheels handle bumps better; smaller wheels give more precise control on smooth surfaces.

- **Tire Material**: Rubberized vs. solid plastic. Look for traction needs.
- **Motor Specs**: DC motors with gearboxes or stepper motors. Choose torque to handle slopes and loads.

11.2.3 Manipulators (Arms, Grippers)

If your robot needs to **pick objects**, design or select a suitable arm or gripper:

- **Simple Gripper**: Two or three-finger designs with a servo or small DC motor.
- **Articulated Arm**: Multiple joints for extended reach or complex manipulation tasks.
- **Sensors on Arm**: Force sensors to avoid crushing objects; encoders for precise joint angles.

11.2.4 Mechanical Integration

Basic Mobile Robot Chassis

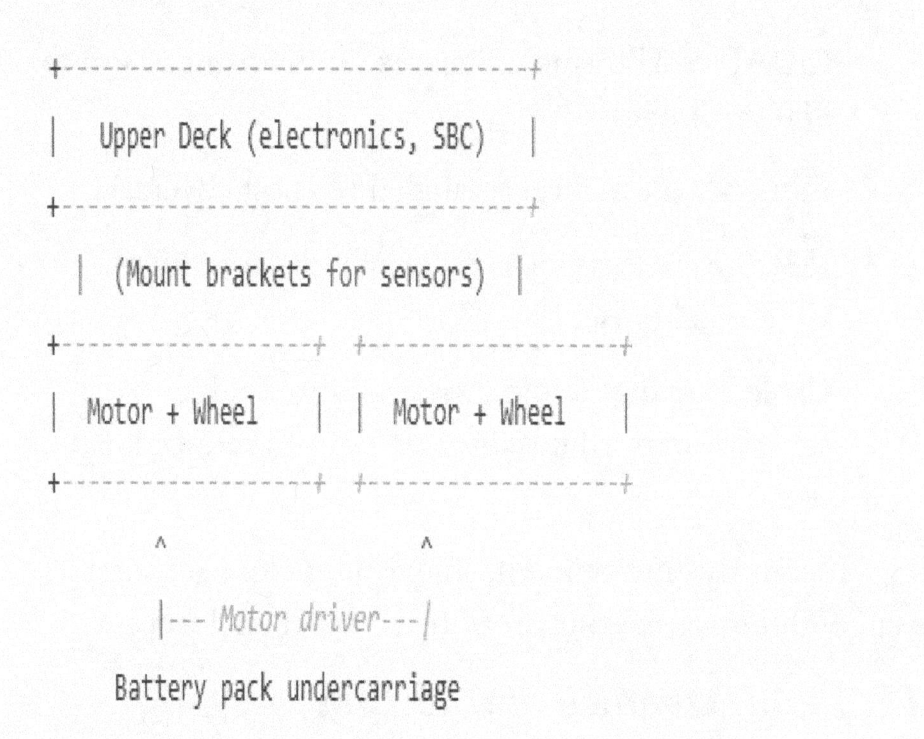

This simplified representation helps visualize where key components (batteries, motors, electronics) might fit.

11.3. Integrating All Systems: Sensors, Navigation, Behaviors

With a sturdy mechanical foundation, the next step is merging **sensing**, **control**, and **high-level behaviors**. This integration is where your knowledge of ROS2 and Python truly shines.

11.3.1 Sensor Placement and Mounting

- **LiDAR or Ultrasonic Sensors** on the front or top for 360° scanning.
- **Cameras** at eye-level or angled for best coverage.
- **IMU** near the robot's center of gravity, reducing vibrational noise.
- **Cable Routing:** Avoid crossing power cables over sensitive sensor lines. Secure wires to reduce tangling or strain.

Tip: In a dusty environment, shield or enclose sensors; in wet conditions, use waterproof or IP-rated enclosures.

11.3.2 Electronics and Wiring

Core Steps:

1. **Microcontroller / Single-Board Computer:** Raspberry Pi, NVIDIA Jetson, or Arduino-based boards.
2. **Motor Drivers:** H-bridge modules or specialized drivers that handle the current demands of your motors.
3. **Power Distribution:** A regulated 5V/12V rail for electronics. Ensure battery capacity matches your required runtime.

4. **Safety:** Fuses or circuit breakers to prevent damage in case of short circuits.

Electrical Integration

```
Battery Pack -> DC-DC Converter -> 5V line -> SBC (like Raspberry Pi)
                        |                \
                        v                 \
                    12V line ----------> Motor Driver -> Motors
Sensors (LiDAR, IMU, etc.) ----------> SBC (via USB/GPIO)
```

11.3.3 ROS2 Nodes: Architecture

1. **Motor Control Node:** Publishes or subscribes to velocity commands (like /cmd_vel) and translates them into PWM signals for motors.
2. **Sensor Nodes:** LiDAR node publishes /scan, camera node publishes /camera/image_raw, etc.
3. **Navigation Stack:** Nav2 for path planning, obstacle avoidance, with messages on topics like /odom, /map, /cmd_vel.
4. **High-Level Behavior:** A Python node running a **state machine** or **behavior tree** decides whether to explore, deliver items, or idle.

Analogy: *Think of your robot as a small company: sensors supply data (R&D), the navigation stack is the operations department making route decisions, the motor control executes tasks (manufacturing), while the high-level behavior node is the CEO deciding overall strategy.*

11.3.4 Testing at Each Stage

- **Electronics Bench Test:** Power up boards, confirm voltage levels, check for short circuits.
- **Sensor Output Verification:** Echo LiDAR topics in rviz to ensure a correct scan.
- **Basic Movement:** Manually publish /cmd_vel messages to confirm motor rotation and direction.
- **Fusion:** Gradually combine pieces (e.g., IMU + wheel odometry + LiDAR) for an integrated navigation test.

11.4. Hands-On Project: A Full Mobile Robot Build with ROS2 and Python

Now we'll walk through a **sample project** that implements these design principles. Our goal is a **differential-drive robot** that can:

- Autonomously navigate using a 2D LiDAR.
- Perform basic object detection with a camera.
- Operate on battery power for about 2 hours.

- Run ROS2 (e.g., Foxy or Humble) and Python for control logic.

11.4.1 Bill of Materials

1. **Chassis:**
    - Aluminum or acrylic platform, 30cm x 25cm.
    - 2 DC motors with encoders.
    - 2 rubber wheels + 1 caster.
2. **Electronics:**
    - Raspberry Pi 4 (4GB or 8GB RAM).
    - 12V Li-ion battery (e.g., ~5000mAh).
    - Motor driver (L298N or TB6612FNG).
    - LiDAR (e.g., RPLIDAR A1 or A2).
    - USB camera (optional, for object detection).
3. **Sensors:**
    - IMU (e.g., MPU6050 or BNO055).
    - Wheel encoders (if your motors don't have built-in ones).
4. **ROS2 Software:**
    - nav2 stack.
    - camera drivers.
    - Python scripts for custom behaviors.

11.4.2 Mechanical Assembly

1. **Mounting Motors:** Bolt DC motors to the underside of the chassis. Ensure alignment so wheels don't wobble.
2. **Wheels and Caster:** Attach wheels to motor shafts, add a caster at the rear.
3. **Sensor Placement:**
    - LiDAR up top or centered so it can sweep 360° if needed.
    - IMU near chassis center.
    - Camera at front, possibly angled up slightly.
4. **Battery Placement:** Under the main platform or behind the motors. Secure it with velcro or brackets for easy swap.

Example Robot Layout

```
+-----------------------------------+
|   LiDAR  |    RPi + Motor Driver   |
|   (top)  |  (center, standoffs)   |
+----------+-----------------------+
        Wheel (left)   Wheel (right)
               [Motor]        [Motor]

            [Caster in rear]
        [Battery pack underneath or back]
```

11.4.3 Wiring and Electronics Setup

1. **Power**:
    - Connect battery to a DC-DC regulator providing stable 5V to the Raspberry Pi.
    - For motors, feed the motor driver from the battery's nominal voltage (e.g., 9-12V).
2. **Signal Lines**:
    - Raspberry Pi GPIO pins to motor driver inputs (e.g., IN1, IN2 for left motor, IN3, IN4 for right motor).
    - ENA/ENB or PWM pins for speed control.
3. **LiDAR**: Connect via USB or serial port.
4. **Camera**: Connect to a USB port or Pi Camera interface if using a Pi camera module.
5. **IMU**: I2C lines to Pi's SDA/SCL pins (with proper pull-up resistors if needed).

11.4.4 Software: ROS2 Packages and Python Nodes

Node 1: Motor Controller

- Subscribes to /cmd_vel for velocity commands.
- Converts linear.x, angular.z into left/right motor speeds.

- Publishes wheel encoder data to /odom for odometry.

Node 2: LiDAR Publisher

- Usually provided by vendor's driver package (e.g., rplidar_ros2).
- Publishes /scan.

Node 3: IMU

- A Python node using an I2C library (like smbus2), publishing orientation data to /imu.

Node 4: Camera

- Could be v4l2_camera or cv_camera package, publishing /image_raw.
- Optional: A custom node to detect simple objects (like ArUco markers or color blobs).

Nav2 Launch

- A launch file that starts amcl or slam_toolbox, costmap, and controller servers.
- Uses sensor topics for obstacle avoidance.

Behavior / High-Level Node

- Optional Python node with a **behavior tree** or **FSM** handling tasks like "Patrol," "Dock to charge," "Chase color object," etc.

11.4.5 Bringing It All Together

1. **Build:**
   - Assemble chassis, wire electronics, verify no short circuits.
   - Boot Raspberry Pi with ROS2 installed.
2. **Test in Stages:**
   - Motor Node: Publish random /cmd_vel to see if wheels spin correctly.
   - LiDAR Node: ros2 topic echo /scan or visualize in RViz.
   - IMU Node: ros2 topic echo /imu to ensure data is stable.
3. **Install Nav2:**

```bash
sudo apt-get update
sudo apt-get install ros-<distro>-nav2-bringup
```

4. **Configure:**
   - Create a params.yaml for Nav2, setting the scan topic, odometry source, etc.
   - Launch Nav2 and try a small navigation test in a known area.

5. **Refine:** Adjust wheel radius, track width, or LiDAR settings. Add collision detection or advanced behaviors as needed.

11.5. Testing, Iterating, and Learning from Failures

Robotics rarely works flawlessly on the first try. **Testing** and **iteration** are the bedrock of building a robust system.

11.5.1 Types of Testing

1. **Unit Tests:** Validate each node or function in isolation (e.g., motor control logic).
2. **Integration Tests:** Combine multiple nodes (motor + LiDAR + navigation) and see if they cooperate correctly.
3. **Field Tests:** Real-world usage in the intended environment (office hallway, workshop floor).

11.5.2 Common Pitfalls and Solutions

- **Motor Power Issues:** Robot doesn't move or motors stall. Check battery voltage and driver current ratings. Possibly gear down for more torque.
- **Sensor Noise:** LiDAR returns ghost points, IMU drifts heavily. Add filters (e.g., EKF) or physically dampen vibrations.

- **Odometry Drift**: The robot strays from its path over time. Re-check wheel circumference, ensure slip is minimized, consider sensor fusion with IMU.
- **Overheating**: SBC or motor driver might overheat if enclosed without proper ventilation. Add fans or heat sinks.

Iterative Testing Cycle

```
[ Prototype Build ] -> [ Basic Tests ] -> [ Identify Issues ]
        ^                                         |
        |                                         v
        [ Redesign / Adjust ] <- [ Field Trials / Integration Tests ]
```

11.5.3 Iteration: Continuous Improvement

1. **Collect Data**: Keep logs (rosbags, CSVs) of sensor outputs, errors, or performance metrics (battery life, CPU usage).
2. **Analyze**: Spot patterns—like a repeated drop in LiDAR data near shiny surfaces or an IMU spike when turning quickly.
3. **Modify**: Tweak mechanical layout, update code, or refine parameter settings in your launch files.
4. **Test Again**: Rinse and repeat until performance meets your needs.

11.5.4 Celebrate Small Wins

When the robot first responds to a /cmd_vel command or you see a LiDAR scan appear in RViz, **take a moment** to appreciate that milestone. Building a robot from scratch is often more complex than it appears, and each success sets the stage for the next challenge.

Conclusion of Chapter 11

Building a **complete robot** from concept to physical hardware and software integration demands a holistic mindset. From **mechanical design** and **electronics** to **ROS2** nodes and iterative **testing**, each step influences the others. A misalignment of your wheels could affect navigation accuracy; an underpowered battery might cause sensor brownouts; or an incomplete software approach could hamper otherwise excellent hardware.

Key Takeaways

1. **Start With Clear Goals**: Understand exactly what you want your robot to do and the constraints you must respect (budget, environment, etc.).
2. **Mechanical Foundations Matter**: A sturdy chassis, correct wheel choice, and well-placed sensors prevent many future problems.

3. **Systems Integration**: Combine hardware, electronics, and ROS2 software carefully, verifying each subsystem independently before merging them.
4. **Hands-On Project Approach**: A step-by-step build ensures that you always have a workable robot, even if not all features are fully implemented yet.
5. **Iterate and Learn**: Embrace testing and accept failures as stepping stones to a robust final product.

Frequently Asked Questions

1. **Q**: Do I need CAD experience to design a chassis?
   A: It helps for more complex builds, but many hobbyists start with off-the-shelf kits or simple platforms. Over time, learning CAD (e.g., Fusion 360, FreeCAD) is invaluable.
2. **Q**: How do I select a motor driver for my motors?
   A: Check the motor's stall current (the highest current it can draw) and voltage range. Choose a driver that can handle more than that stall current for a safety margin.
3. **Q**: Is LiDAR mandatory for navigation?
   A: Not always. Some robots use only ultrasonic or depth cameras. However, LiDAR is a common choice for reliable 2D scanning and straightforward integration with Nav2.
4. **Q**: How can I automate tasks like picking up or dropping objects?

A: Use a gripper controlled by servos or stepper motors, and add feedback sensors if needed. Integrate this manipulator node with your main behavior or state machine.

5. **Q**: What if my environment is mostly outdoors or has rough terrain?
   A: Consider larger wheels, higher torque motors, maybe a suspension system or tracked design, plus sensor solutions that handle bright sunlight (e.g., a 3D LiDAR or RTK GPS for localization).

What's Next?

You've now grasped how to **conceptualize**, **design**, **assemble**, and **iterate** on a full robot project. From here, you might explore:

- **Advanced Manipulation**: Adding a multi-joint robotic arm or advanced gripper with force sensing.
- **Multi-Robot Systems**: Coordinating multiple robots, each running ROS2, for tasks like warehouse swarming or search-and-rescue.
- **AI & Machine Learning**: Integrating real-time object detection, voice interaction, or reinforcement learning strategies to push autonomy further.

The next step is to pick a project—**maybe even the one we outlined here**—and make it your own. Remember, the best way to learn robotics is by **doing**, failing fast, and evolving your design with each iteration. Good luck, and have fun building your custom ROS2-powered robot!

Chapter 12: Troubleshooting and Maintenance

No matter how meticulously you build your robot's hardware or craft your ROS2 nodes, **problems** will inevitably arise. The real question is how swiftly and effectively you can diagnose and fix them. This chapter zeroes in on **common pitfalls** and offers a structured guide to **maintenance**—covering everything from daily checklists to advanced diagnostics. By honing your troubleshooting skills, you'll keep your robot running smoothly, extend its lifespan, and glean valuable lessons for continuous improvement.

From code-level bugs to hardware malfunctions, let's break down how to **detect**, **debug**, and **prevent** the most common issues in robotics.

12.1. Common ROS2 and Python Errors and Their Solutions

When working with **ROS2** and **Python**, a range of errors can pop up—from missing dependencies to environment misconfigurations. Below, we'll highlight some frequent culprits and outline practical fixes.

12.1.1 ROS2 Environment and Setup Issues

1. **"Command 'ros2' not found"**
    - **Cause:** Your ROS2 environment isn't sourced, or you installed ROS2 in a different shell session.
    - **Solution:**
        1. Ensure you add a line in your ~/.bashrc or shell profile:

```bash
source /opt/ros/<distro>/setup.bash
```

        2. In a fresh terminal, verify by running which ros2.
        3. If you have multiple ROS2 distributions, confirm you're sourcing the correct one.

2. **"Package '[pkg_name]' not found"**
    - **Cause:** The package wasn't built or the workspace setup wasn't sourced.
    - **Solution:**
        1. Inside your workspace, run:

```bash
colcon build
source install/setup.bash
```

2. Check package.xml for missing <build_depend> or <exec_depend> tags.
3. Confirm correct package names in ros2 pkg list.

3. **"Could not contact service /rosout"**
   - **Cause:** The core ROS2 services didn't launch or crashed.
   - **Solution:**
     1. Restart the terminal or kill any leftover processes.
     2. Run ros2 doctor --report to see if core nodes are active.
     3. Re-check if you're mixing multiple ROS2 installations.

12.1.2 Python-Specific Pitfalls

1. **ImportErrors / ModuleNotFoundError**
   - **Cause:** Missing Python dependencies or incorrect $PYTHONPATH.
   - **Solution:**
     1. Install dependencies: pip install <package_name> or sudo apt-get install python3-<package>.

2. If using a virtual environment, ensure you activated it:

```bash
source ~/venv/ros2/bin/activate
```

2. **SyntaxError / IndentationError**
   - **Cause:** Mistakes in Python code, such as mismatched indentation or invalid syntax.
   - **Solution:**
     1. Use a code editor with Python syntax highlighting.
     2. Run static checks: flake8 or pylint on your code.
3. **RuntimeError: dictionary changed size during iteration**
   - **Cause:** Modifying a dictionary or list while iterating over it.
   - **Solution:**
     1. Copy or listify the keys before iterating if you must modify them.
     2. Example fix:

```python
for k in list(my_dict.keys()):
    if condition(my_dict[k]):
```

```
del my_dict[k]
```

4. **GIL / Performance Bottlenecks**
   - **Cause:** CPU-bound tasks in Python blocked by the Global Interpreter Lock.
   - **Solution:**
     1. Use multiprocessing or offload heavy tasks to C++ or GPU libraries.
     2. Profile code with cProfile or py-spy to find slow sections.

12.1.3 Colcon Build and Dependency Woes

1. **Build Fails with "Could not find a package configuration file"**
   - **Cause:** A missing or incorrect dependency in package.xml or CMakeLists.txt.
   - **Solution:**
     1. Double-check you have declared dependencies properly, for instance <build_depend>ament_cmake_ros</build_depend>.
     2. If using a third-party library, ensure it's installed system-wide or in your workspace.
2. **Linker Errors or "undefined reference"**

- **Cause**: In C++ nodes, you might have missed linking a library.
- **Solution**:
    1. Add the library via target_link_libraries or ament_target_dependencies.
    2. Ensure the library is installed on your system or built in the same workspace.

12.2. Diagnosing Hardware Issues (Voltage, Connections, Sensor Malfunctions)

Mechanical or electrical mishaps can ground even the best software. Let's explore a methodical approach to diagnosing **hardware** troubles.

12.2.1 Step-by-Step Hardware Diagnosis

1. **Visual Inspection**:
    - Check for loose wires, burnt components, or bent pins.
    - Ensure connectors are firmly seated—vibration can jar them loose over time.
2. **Multimeter Testing**:

  - Confirm voltage levels at your power supply rails (5V, 12V).
  - Check continuity on ground lines. A missing ground reference can cause erratic behavior.

3. **Load Testing:**
   - If motors stall, measure current draw. Is it exceeding your motor driver's rating?
   - Does your battery voltage drop significantly under load?
4. **Sensor Self-Tests:**
   - Many sensors (IMU, LiDAR) include diagnostic info in their data streams. For instance, LiDAR might return an error code if it can't spin freely.

12.2.2 Common Electrical Faults

1. **Overheating Regulators:** If your voltage regulator gets too hot to touch, it may be overloaded. Consider a higher current regulator or add a heat sink.
2. **Brownouts:** If your single-board computer (like a Raspberry Pi) reboots when motors start, the supply might be dipping below 5V. Upgrade your power supply or separate motor and logic rails.
3. **Noise Interference:** High-current lines near sensor wires can introduce electromagnetic interference.

Route cables with separation or use shielded cables. Add ferrite beads for extra noise suppression.

12.2.3 Sensor Malfunctions

1. **No Data on Sensor Topic:**
   - Check dmesg or Windows Device Manager to see if the sensor enumerates as a serial/USB device.
   - Is the correct port specified in your launch file or code?
2. **Inaccurate Data:**
   - Calibrate sensors, especially IMUs or cameras.
   - Use a known reference object or environment to verify measurements.
   - Watch for temperature or mechanical stress that shifts sensor readings.

Basic Electrical Troubleshooting Flow

```
[Check Power Rails] -> stable 5V, 12V?

    | No -> fix supply/regulators

    | Yes

    v

[Check Connections] -> loose wires? reversed polarity?

    | No issues found

    v

[Test Sensor Individually] -> read raw data in isolation

    | If fails -> replace or calibrate sensor

    v

[Reintegrate, Monitor for Overloads or Noise]
```

12.3. Monitoring and Logging in ROS2

Proactive monitoring helps spot anomalies before they become failures. ROS2 offers built-in tools for logging, introspection, and data recording that can be vital for debugging.

12.3.1 ROS2 Logging

Each ROS2 node can produce **log messages** at various severity levels:

- **DEBUG**: Detailed output for developers.
- **INFO**: Routine messages about the robot's status.
- **WARN**: Non-critical issues that may indicate problems if not addressed.
- **ERROR**: Serious issues that might stop the robot from performing tasks.
- **FATAL**: Crashes or conditions that force immediate shutdown.

Example (Python snippet):

```
python


import rclpy
from rclpy.node import Node


class MyNode(Node):
    def __init__(self):
        super().__init__('my_node')
        self.get_logger().info("Node started
successfully")
        # ...
        self.get_logger().warn("Low battery
detected")


def main():
    rclpy.init()
    node = MyNode()
```

```
rclpy.spin(node)
node.destroy_node()
rclpy.shutdown()
```

12.3.2 Real-Time Introspection: ros2 topic, ros2 node

- **ros2 node list**: Check which nodes are running.
- **ros2 topic echo /topic_name**: See live data from sensors or other publishers.
- **ros2 topic hz /topic_name**: Monitor publishing frequency.

12.3.3 Recording Data with ros2 bag

ros2 bag lets you **record** all or selected topics for replay later, enabling offline analysis of sensor data and debugging.

1. **Recording**:

```
bash

ros2 bag record -a
```

This captures all topics. Alternatively, specify particular topics to narrow data volume.

2. **Playing**:

```
bash

ros2 bag play <bagfile>
```

This replays topics as if they were live, perfect for analyzing or developing solutions offline.

12.3.4 Visualization with RViZ

RViZ remains a cornerstone of ROS-based debugging:

- **TF frames**: Check if coordinate transforms match expectations (e.g., odom, base_link, camera_link).
- **LiDAR scans**: Visualize obstacles or missing data patches.
- **Robot Model**: Confirm sensors or robot arms appear in the right positions.

12.4. Creating a Maintenance Checklist: Preventative Measures

A well-maintained robot is more reliable, safer, and cheaper to operate over the long haul. Let's compile a standard maintenance checklist that covers mechanical, electrical, and software aspects.

12.4.1 Daily or Pre-Run Checks

1. **Battery Levels**: Ensure adequate charge; check for swelling or damage on LiPo or Li-ion packs.
2. **Visual Inspection**: Loose screws, worn tires, or tangled cables.

3. **Sensor Cleanliness:** Wipe LiDAR or camera lenses to remove dust or smudges.

12.4.2 Weekly or Monthly Checks

1. **Firmware Updates:** Microcontroller or sensor firmware might fix bugs or add features.
2. **Calibration Review:** IMU or camera calibrations can drift over time or after mechanical shock.
3. **Lubrication / Belt Tension:** For mechanical parts or arms, follow manufacturer recommendations.

12.4.3 Software Housekeeping

1. **Log Rotation:** Too many large logs can eat disk space, especially if you record high-frequency sensor data.
2. **ROS2 Package Upgrades:** Periodically run sudo apt-get update && sudo apt-get upgrade or rebuild from source if needed.
3. **Security Patches:** If your robot is networked, keep the OS and libraries patched.

12.4.4 Spare Parts and Tools

- **Backup Sensors:** A spare LiDAR or camera, in case of field failures.
- **Fuses / Connectors:** Quick replacements for blown fuses or broken connectors.

- **Common Tools:** A small kit with screwdrivers, multimeter, and cable ties ensures quick repairs.

Example Maintenance Checklist

```
|---------------|-------------------------|
|  Frequency    |          Tasks          |
|---------------|-------------------------|
| Daily         | 1) Check battery        |
| (Pre-run)     | 2) Inspect wiring       |
|               | 3) Wipe sensors         |
|---------------|-------------------------|
| Weekly        | 1) Firmware updates     |
| /Monthly      | 2) Re-calibrate IMU     |
|               | 3) Verify logs/disk     |
|---------------|-------------------------|
```

12.5. Best Practices for Continuous Improvement

Finally, let's cover how to **evolve** your system and processes over time, ensuring each iteration of your robot is more refined than the last.

12.5.1 Embrace a "Kaizen" Mindset

"Kaizen" is a Japanese term meaning **continuous improvement**. Applied to robotics:

1. **Always Seek Feedback**: Ask operators or teammates for issues they face. Watch for usage patterns that cause problems.
2. **Regular Retrospectives**: After each big test or deployment, note what went well and what didn't.
3. **Incremental Upgrades**: Instead of massive overhauls, add or refine features step by step—this reduces risk.

12.5.2 Track Performance Metrics

Record data like:

- **CPU / Memory Usage**: Identify if nodes are hogging resources.
- **Navigation Success Rate**: Count how often the robot fails or gets stuck.
- **Battery Endurance**: Log time from full charge to depletion under typical loads.
- **Mean Time Between Failures (MTBF)**: Over weeks or months, track how frequently breakdowns occur, then target the biggest issues.

12.5.3 Document Everything

Clear documentation ensures future you (or another developer) can quickly pick up where you left off:

1. **Hardware Schematics**: Store them in your repository or a shared drive.
2. **Configuration Files**: Keep YAML and launch files versioned in Git.
3. **Troubleshooting Logs**: Maintain a wiki or README describing known errors and solutions, so you don't solve the same problems repeatedly.

12.5.4 Collaborative Improvement

If you're part of a team:

- **Code Reviews**: Even for Python scripts, a second pair of eyes can catch logic errors or style inconsistencies.
- **Pair Debugging**: Two people at one console can often pinpoint issues faster.
- **User Community**: For open-source packages, contribute bug fixes or enhancements back to the community. A robust community reciprocates with more stable libraries and solutions.

Continuous Improvement Loop

```
      [ Observe & Log Data ]
               |
               v
    [ Analyze Failures & Metrics ]
               |
               v
      [ Implement Small Fixes ]
               |
               v
    [ Test & Collect Feedback ]
               |
              ...
```

This cyclical process ensures each iteration yields a more robust, efficient robot.

Conclusion of Chapter 12

Even the best-designed robots will encounter hiccups—**hardware malfunctions**, **software glitches**, and **environmental surprises**. An engineer's ability to systematically **troubleshoot**, **maintain**, and **continuously improve** is the difference between persistent frustration and a reliable, high-performing system. This chapter has laid out:

1. **Common ROS2 and Python Errors**: How to spot and fix them quickly, from environment misconfigurations to build script headaches.
2. **Hardware Diagnostics**: Practical methods for uncovering voltage drops, motor driver overloads, or failing sensors.
3. **Monitoring & Logging**: Tools like ros2 bag, RViZ, and built-in logging facilities for real-time introspection.
4. **Maintenance Checklists**: Proactive steps—daily, weekly, monthly—to keep your robot in peak condition.
5. **Continuous Improvement**: Strategies to refine your robotics system over time, ensuring each iteration is more dependable than the last.

Key Takeaways

- **Debugging**: Tackle issues methodically—start simple, isolate variables, and confirm each layer (power, sensors, software) is working as intended.
- **Logging & Monitoring**: Leverage ROS2's built-in tools to spot anomalies early.
- **Preventative Maintenance**: A little effort on a regular basis can prevent catastrophic failures.
- **Data-Driven Iteration**: Gather logs, analyze trends, and steadily refine your design.

- **Team Collaboration:** Shared knowledge through documentation, code reviews, and open communication speeds up resolution and fosters innovation.

Frequently Asked Questions

1. **Q**: Is there a command to automatically fix environment issues in ROS2?
   A: Not exactly. Tools like ros2 doctor help diagnose common pitfalls but can't fix them all. You usually have to adjust your shell config, install missing packages, or correct your build.
2. **Q**: What if a sensor is physically damaged?
   A: Replace it or attempt repairs if feasible. Keep spares on hand, especially for crucial components like LiDAR or cameras.
3. **Q**: Are real-time logs from Python nodes going to slow down my system?
   A: Excessive debug logs can degrade performance slightly. Use log levels wisely (INFO for normal ops, DEBUG for deep dives).
4. **Q**: How do I handle partial sensor data or intermittent connectivity?
   A: Implement fallback logic or a fusion node that gracefully degrades if one sensor feed drops. Also use network monitoring or robust QoS profiles for remote connections.

5. **Q**: Does "continuous improvement" mean I'll never be done with my robot?
   A: In a way, yes! Robotics is iterative—technology advances, your needs evolve, and new obstacles arise. Embrace that each iteration is a step toward a more capable, resilient machine.

What's Next?

With a foundation in **troubleshooting** and **maintenance**, you're armed to keep your robotics projects alive, evolving, and pushing boundaries. The upcoming final chapters tie together everything we've learned—offering a **roadmap** for future exploration, advanced AI integrations, and ways to stay connected with the global ROS2 and Python community. Remember, every glitch is an **opportunity** to refine your design, deepen your understanding, and create an even more impressive robot tomorrow.

Chapter 13: The Road Ahead—Research, Innovation, and Future Directions

You've ventured through a complete curriculum of robotics—covering sensors, navigation, behavior design, and even hardware builds. But where do you go from here? Robotics is a rapidly evolving field, with **ROS2** at its core, driving new frontiers in **AI**, **edge computing**, and multi-robot collaboration. In this final chapter, we'll explore the **next wave** of ROS2 features, highlight how **machine learning** is transforming robotics, discuss opportunities to **engage** with competitions and communities, delve into **cloud** and **edge** innovations, and wrap up with some heartfelt words of **encouragement**.

By the end, you'll have a vision of **what's next**—both for you as a robotics innovator and for the worldwide ROS2 community.

13.1. What's Next for ROS2?

ROS2 has matured considerably, evolving from its early distributions (Ardent, Bouncy) into robust, industry-ready releases like **Humble**, **Iron**, and beyond. Each iteration polishes core features, refines performance, and cements **DDS** underpinnings. But the story isn't over. Here's a glimpse of **future directions** and active developments.

13.1.1 Real-Time Enhancements

1. **Improved Scheduling**: Community-driven efforts (e.g., real-time kernels or specialized scheduling frameworks) aim to reduce jitter and latency for high-frequency loops (such as robotic arms or drones).
2. **Lifecycle Nodes**: Future expansions of lifecycle management could automate fault recovery and node restarts for systems needing 24/7 uptime.
3. **RTOS Integration**: We might see deeper ties with real-time operating systems, ensuring even tighter control loops.

13.1.2 Expanded Platform Support

1. **Embedded Systems**: Tools like **micro-ROS** keep pushing boundaries, letting microcontrollers run ROS2-like features.
2. **GPU Acceleration**: Expect more official examples harnessing CUDA or OpenCL for accelerating heavy tasks like point cloud processing or neural inference.
3. **Windows and macOS**: While Linux remains the gold standard, better cross-platform support helps developers code on whichever OS they prefer.

13.1.3 Richer Ecosystem of Plugins and Tools

1. **Nav2**: Continuous improvements in path planning, costmap layers, and multi-robot collaboration.
2. **Sensor Drivers**: More plug-and-play drivers for new LiDARs, depth cameras, or custom IMUs.
3. **Security & Encryption**: Enhanced tools for encryption at rest and in transit, vital for enterprise or military-grade robots.

Potential Evolution of ROS2

```
Future ROS2
   |----- Real-Time Kernel Integration
   |----- Micro-ROS for Microcontrollers
   |----- Enhanced Security (DDS-level)
   |----- GPU-Accelerated Modules
   +---> A More Seamless Robot Operating System
```

13.1.4 Community and Governance

As ROS2 transitions from Open Robotics stewardship to a broader open-source model, the community's voice drives priorities. Whether you're a developer, researcher, or hobbyist, **contributing** bug reports, merges, or new packages is how you can shape the roadmap. Keep an eye on the **ROS Discourse** forums and official announcements.

13.2. AI and Machine Learning in Robotics

Robotics and AI are **converging** rapidly, producing machines that can **learn** from data, adapt to new environments, and even reason about tasks in human-like ways. Let's explore the intersection points and how you can capitalize on them.

13.2.1 ML-Driven Perception

Robots rely on **vision, LiDAR**, and other sensors to build a world model. Conventional algorithms (like edge detection or feature matching) have their limits. Today's cutting-edge solutions use **convolutional neural networks** (CNNs) or **transformers** to:

1. **Detect Objects**: Identify and track dynamic obstacles in real-time.
2. **Segment Scenes**: Label floor vs. walls vs. furniture, enabling robust path planning.
3. **Pose Estimation**: Understand how humans or manipulators are positioned to interact safely.

13.2.2 Reinforcement Learning (RL)

RL trains a robot by **trial and error**, rewarding successful actions (like stable walking or precise picking). This approach is used in advanced tasks:

1. **Dexterous Manipulation**: RL can refine a robotic hand's grip strategy.
2. **Navigation**: Some robots learn to map from sensor data directly to velocity commands.
3. **Multi-Agent Systems**: RL fosters collaborative behaviors among multiple robots, learning tactics that surpass direct programming.

13.2.3 Integrating ML with ROS2

1. **ROS2 Packages**: Tools like ros2_trt_pose or ros2_tensorflow can accelerate deep learning in Python nodes.
2. **Hardware Acceleration**: NVIDIA Jetson boards or Intel Movidius sticks speed up neural net inference at the edge.
3. **Training vs. Inference**: Typically, you train big models offline (in Python or specialized frameworks), then deploy minimal inference nodes on the robot.

13.2.4 AI Challenges

- **Data Collection:** Creating large, labeled datasets can be time-consuming. Synthetic data from simulation might help but can misrepresent real-world noise.
- **Model Size:** Neural networks can be heavy on memory and compute. Pruning, quantization, or specialized hardware can mitigate these constraints.
- **Robustness:** ML can behave unpredictably in out-of-distribution environments (e.g., new lighting conditions or unexpected obstacles).

AI Integration in a ROS2 System

```
Sensors (Images, LiDAR)
   -> ML Node (Object Detector, CNN)
   -> /detected_objects
            |
            v
  Nav Stack (Nav2)
  merges /detected_objects
  with costmaps -> updated path
```

13.3. Robotics Competitions and Community Involvement

Competitions spark innovation, push boundaries, and help you refine skills under pressure. Meanwhile, active **community** involvement expands your network and knowledge base. Let's look at ways to plug in.

13.3.1 Popular Competitions

1. **RoboCup**: Focuses on robot soccer, rescue tasks, and industrial automation challenges.
2. **FIRST Robotics**: Inspires K-12 students with team-based engineering challenges. Mentoring a FIRST team can sharpen your teaching and design skills.
3. **DARPA Challenges**: Historically spurred huge leaps in autonomous vehicles and disaster response. Keep an eye out for ongoing or future government-sponsored contests.
4. **Eurobot, RoboMaster, IMAV**: Region-specific competitions with varied scopes—everything from aerial swarms to manipulator tasks.

13.3.2 ROS2-Focused Hackathons

Many conferences (ROSCon, ICRA, etc.) host **hackathons** or "code sprints" where teams converge to solve ROS2-related problems:

- **Community Projects**: Tackle driver integration, build new Nav2 plugins, or refine simulation environments.
- **Lightning Collaboration**: Rapid prototyping with strangers turned teammates can yield lasting connections.

13.3.3 Benefits of Engaging

- **Motivation**: Deadlines and competitive spirit keep you pushing forward.
- **Peer Learning**: Competitions expose you to new hardware, code patterns, and best practices from other teams.
- **Networking**: Sponsors, companies, and potential collaborators often scout these events.

Step-by-Step to Get Involved:

1. Identify a competition that matches your interests (e.g., mobile robots, drones, manipulation).
2. Form or join a local team—check university clubs or Meetup groups.
3. Plan a project timeline: design, build, test, iterate.
4. Document everything—competitions often reward well-explained solutions, not just raw performance.
5. After the event, reflect on lessons learned and consider open-sourcing your code.

13.4. Leveraging Cloud Robotics and Edge Computing

Robotics is no longer confined to on-board controllers. With **cloud robotics** and **edge computing**, you can distribute intelligence across a network, combining local real-time control with powerful remote processing.

13.4.1 Why Cloud Robotics?

1. **Heavy Computation Offloading**: Advanced AI or large-scale mapping can run in the cloud, freeing up local CPU/GPU resources.
2. **Global Data Sharing**: A fleet of robots can share maps, object recognizers, or learned behaviors in a central repository.
3. **Scalable**: Spin up more cloud instances for intense tasks, scaling down when idle to save costs.

13.4.2 Edge Computing Advantages

1. **Low Latency**: Real-time tasks (like obstacle avoidance) can't wait for cloud round trips. Edge devices handle critical decisions locally.
2. **Reduced Bandwidth**: Not all sensor data needs to stream to the cloud. Summaries or processed insights suffice, saving bandwidth.
3. **Resilience**: If the network goes down, edge computing keeps core operations alive.

13.4.3 Hybrid Architecture

Hybrid Robot Architecture

```
On-Robot SBC (Edge)
 +---LiDAR, Camera---+
 |  Real-time tasks  |
 |  Nav2, Obstacle   |
 |  Avoidance        |
 +-------------------+
           |
           | (selective data)
           v
  Cloud Server (GPU/AI)
     - ML model training
     - Global map aggregator
     - Fleet management
```

The robot runs key control loops locally (low latency) while uploading logs or partial sensor data to a remote server for advanced analytics, training, or re-planning.

13.4.4 Implementation Tips

1. **MQTT or WebSocket Bridges**: Some set up a ROS2 <-> MQTT or WebSocket interface for the cloud.

2. **Docker/Kubernetes:** Containerize your cloud services, ensuring consistency and easy scaling.
3. **Security:** Use VPNs or secure DDS QoS settings to protect data.
4. **Fallback:** If the network fails, the local system should maintain operational autonomy.

13.5. Final Words of Encouragement

Over the course of this book, we've delved into **ROS2** and **Python** for building sophisticated, intelligent robots. We've seen how they integrate with hardware, manage complex behaviors, enable advanced navigation, and connect with AI or the cloud. Now, standing at the threshold of **infinite** robotic possibilities, it's time to reflect on your journey and look toward the future.

1. **Embrace the Unknown:** Robotics is inherently iterative. Failures are not the end; they're your teachers.
2. **Stay Curious:** Keep exploring new sensors, algorithms, or frameworks—there's always more to learn in robotics.
3. **Collaborate Freely:** The open-source community thrives on sharing knowledge. Contribute bug fixes, answer forum posts, or build your own open hardware designs.

4. **Think Big**: Today's simple mobile robot could evolve into a multi-robot system or even an interplanetary rover. Dare to dream.
5. **Enjoy the Process**: Building, coding, and debugging can be challenging—but each success, no matter how small, is a step toward mastery.

Step-by-Step Inspiration:

1. Pick a domain: **Healthcare**, **manufacturing**, **disaster response**, or something else that sparks your passion.
2. Set a tangible project goal (like "automate corridor patrol in my office").
3. Gather resources: from hardware kits, online tutorials, to local maker communities.
4. Apply your knowledge in real builds. Document each iteration, each triumph, each bug fix.
5. Share your project. Let your robot's story inspire others and invite collaboration.

Remember, **you** have the power to shape the future of robotics. The synergy of robust open-source platforms like ROS2, intuitive languages like Python, and your creativity is driving the field forward at breakneck speed. Whether you're an industry professional, a researcher, or a hobbyist, your contributions—big or small—make a difference. So go forth, build, experiment, fail fast, learn constantly, and watch as your ideas turn into innovations that enrich lives, solve problems, and expand humanity's reach.

www.ingramcontent.com/pod-product-compliance
Lightning Source LLC
LaVergne TN
LVHW080112070326
832902LV00015B/2550
* 9 7 9 8 3 0 9 2 2 2 2 4 7 *